Project Diosdado XI: Taking the Red Pill in the Age of Digital Predators

Reinaldo Aguiar

Published by Reinaldo Aguiar, 2025.

PROJECT DIOSDADO XI: TAKING THE RED PILL IN THE AGE OF DIGITAL PREDATORS

First edition. July 24, 2025.

Copyright © 2025 Reinaldo Aguiar.

ISBN: 979-8999684714

Written by Reinaldo Aguiar.

Table of Contents

Never yield to force; never yield to the apparently overwhelming might of the enemy.

— Winston ChurchillSpeech at Harrow School, October 29, 1941

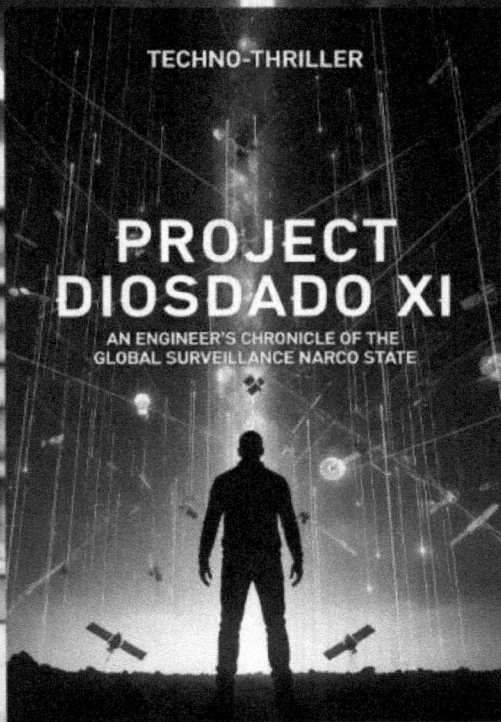

Project Diosdado XI: Taking the Red Pill in the Age of Digital Predators

Author: Reinaldo Aguiar

(Copyright Page)

Project Diosdado XI: Taking the Red Pill in the Age of Digital Predators

Published by Reinaldo Aguiar at Katy, Texas.

ISBN 979-8-9996847-0-7

Russian Federation, the Islamic Republic of Iran, and the Republic of Cuba.

2. This work may not be used by any commercial entity for any purpose intended for commercial advantage, profit generation, or monetary compensation without the express prior written consent of the author.

For all other uses, please contact the publisher.
Email: aguiar@reinaldo.ca
ISBN 979-8-9996847-0-7 (ebook)
ISBN 979-8-9996847-1-4 (paperback)
Version 1.1.0 / July 2025

Disclaimer:

This book is a work of non-fiction. It is a chronicle of the author's personal experiences, memories, and analysis of data collected between 2001 and 2025. The events and conversations in this book are reconstructed to the best of the author's ability. The author and publisher assume no liability for any actions taken by readers based on the information and hypotheses presented herein. The views and theories expressed are those of the author.

(Dedication Page)
For all those who have been silenced,
and for the truth that will not be.

Author's Note

This book is a work of non-fiction based on the author's personal experiences and extensive research.

While the events, individuals, and entities described are real, some names and identifying details may have been altered to protect sources or for narrative clarity.

The core truths of the surveillance, corruption, and technological warfare documented within these pages, however, remain unchanged.

Table of Contents

Part 4: The Internet of Spies

Part 5: The Gauntlet

Afterword: The Second Pill
Appendices

8

Timeline of Events
Index of Characters, Groups, and Entities
Glossary

Resources for Citizens and Law Enforcement Agencies

Introduction

In the iconic 2000s film *The Matrix*, the protagonist is offered a choice: take the blue pill and remain in blissful ignorance within a simulated world, or take the red pill and awaken to the terrifying, raw truth of reality. This book is your red pill. The information contained in these pages will fundamentally alter your perception of the world, society, and the invisible systems of control that govern our lives. This is your opportunity to turn back.

As I unraveled this conspiracy, I realized that what I was witnessing was more than just a criminal enterprise. It was a violation of the natural order. In nature, species protect their young to ensure their own survival. This network, a union of a prior generation of politicians, spies, and technologists, does the opposite. They are **Predators**, actively working to consume and destroy the potential of the next generation to prevent being displaced and to maintain their own power indefinitely.

Their psychology is that of the guards in the famous **Stanford Prison Experiment**: a group of ordinary individuals given unlimited power and no accountability, who inevitably descend into cruelty and sadism. For two decades, they have been playing "Guards" with the rest of the world as their inmates. This book is a chronicle of their experiment, and my fight to end it.

Project Diosdado XI chronicles one software engineer's journey from unwitting surveillance target to sophisticated counter-intelligence operator. Set against the backdrop of suburban Texas, this narrative reveals a global conspiracy involving Venezuelan intelligence services, Chinese state hackers, corrupted corporations, and a vast network of human assets operating as a surveillance narco state.

9

What began as anomalies in my internet connection evolved into the discovery of a criminal enterprise of staggering scope. This book exposes multiple interlocking operations: internet infrastructure compromised at the ISP level, decades-long placement of human intelligence assets, the theft of Google's search algorithm to manipulate global e-commerce, a shadow internet using satellite reflections, targeted biological warfare including attacks on children, systematic corruption of the legal system, and the weaponization of healthcare for intelligence operations.

Through meticulous documentation and technical analysis, I not only survived these attacks but discovered the network's operational database through pattern recognition of physical surveillance. By searching for files containing the exact coordinates where I was repeatedly intercepted while running, I found their hidden geo-index on a French research server. The story culminates with the discovery of the "bigram key"—the encoding system that makes every network vehicle identifiable, transforming anonymous surveillance assets into marked targets for justice.

But this book reveals more than a criminal conspiracy—it exposes a fundamental shift in the nature of warfare itself. The same technologies that enable innovation and connection have been weaponized for surveillance and control. Just as previous generations witnessed the militarization of ships and atoms, we are now witnessing the weaponization of code. The surveillance narco state documented here represents the first implementation of a new form of conflict where software engineers are soldiers, algorithms are ammunition, and entire populations can be enslaved through lines of code.

Written in the clinical, paranoid style of Orwell's "1984," this book serves as both personal memoir and urgent warning. It reveals how authoritarian regimes and criminal networks have merged with technology companies to create unprecedented capabilities for human control—and how those same technologies can be turned against the oppressors. More critically, it exposes the strategic vulnerability facing democratic nations that have failed to recognize software engineering as a matter of national defense.

The narrative asks fundamental questions: How do we maintain human dignity in an age of total surveillance? What happens when those entrusted to protect us become our greatest threat? How can individual technical knowledge combat state-level resources? And most urgently: How can free societies survive when authoritarian regimes are building armies of software engineers while we still train soldiers for yesterday's wars?

The answers lie not in despair but in documentation, analysis, education, and the patient accumulation of evidence. The network believed their technological superiority made them invulnerable. Instead, it made them traceable. Every crime created data. Every operation generated patterns. Every cruelty strengthened the case against them. But lasting victory requires more than exposing one network—it demands a fundamental reimagining of education and defense for the digital age.

Project Diosdado XI is ultimately a story of hope and a call to action—proof that even the most sophisticated surveillance narco state can be exposed by one person with the skills to see patterns, the courage to document them, and the persistence to survive long enough to tell the tale. My goal in presenting this chronicle is not personal revenge; it is to apply my expertise to package these findings in a way that creates a product for justice. A conventional investigation into a conspiracy of this scale could take years, during which time the world would remain a hostage. My hope is that this work will serve to drastically **shorten the investigative timeline** for the real authorities, so that justice may come not only for me, but for the millions they have targeted, and for the future they seek to control. The key has been found. But the war for human freedom in the age of weaponized software has only just begun.

About the Author

Reinaldo Aguiar is a researcher and apprentice tactician with a diverse background spanning software engineering, entrepreneurship, technology, and high finance. His career has focused on improving search technologies and building innovative systems that have generated hundreds of millions in revenue for major corporations.

Prior to creating KeyOpinionLeaders.com and TheSpybusters.com, Reinaldo held several significant roles at major tech companies. At Twitter, he worked as a Software Engineer, focusing on re-architecting the entire Ads-Billing stack, ads-revenue generation, and search improvements. He notably implemented a single code change that increased revenue by $48 million annually—a one-hour modification that earned a personal thank-you from Elon Musk, years before their paths would cross under very different circumstances.

At Goldman Sachs, he served as a Hands-on Managing Director, spearheading the development of a finance-focused search engine and mentoring the firm-wide search team. This work earned the team first place in the Goldman Sachs Accelerate incubator program, demonstrating his ability to bridge the worlds of technology and finance.

Reinaldo is a former Software Engineer at Google, named as sole inventor on two patents awarded by the U.S. Patent Office to Google Inc. The first, USPO Patent #9,275,419, describes a method for building, expanding, or complementing a social graph based on contact information. The second, USPO Patent US-20150205766-A1, details a method for optimizing information transmission between computer systems to minimize payload size and data transfer latency at the transport and application layers. These innovations in data analysis and network optimization would later prove crucial in understanding and exposing the surveillance network's operations.

During the course of the confrontations with Elon Musk, Diosdado Cabello, Pierre Omidyar, Peter Thiel, Travis Kalanick, Vladimir

Padrino López, and the rest of the "PayPal Mafia" that led to the development of the TheSpybusters.com counterintelligence platform, Reinaldo inadvertently received what he describes as daily training for years. This unconventional education came through adversarial contact with some of the world's most sophisticated intelligence services, including the FSB, Iranian Intelligence Services, and the Venezuelan and Cuban Intelligence Services. Even more ironically, patterns in the surveillance suggested indirect influence from figures like Robert Gates, former U.S. Defense Secretary, whose properties appeared in the geo-index with distinctive geographical features that the network replicated at their own facilities.

Currently, Reinaldo dedicates his time to developing counterintelligence software to expose the PayPal Mafia's alleged criminal activities and engaging in digital activism. He advocates for increased regulation of the technology industry, greater cooperation between nations in cybersecurity matters, and more coordinated international oversight of technology platforms and the internet as a whole.

Most urgently, he champions the prioritization of software engineering in Western educational systems as a matter of national defense. Having witnessed firsthand how adversarial nations have weaponized software development—turning code into tools of surveillance and control—he warns that the West faces a critical shortage of defensive capability. While at Google Search, he observed that the engineering teams were dominated by Chinese, Russian, and Indian engineers, with almost no American or Hispanic representation. This imbalance, he argues, represents a strategic vulnerability as profound as any military gap. Just as nations once built navies after realizing ships could carry cannons, and nuclear arsenals after discovering atomic weapons, countries like China are now building armies of software engineers after recognizing that code itself is a weapon. Without a comparable investment in technical education and talent development, democratic nations risk being overwhelmed by authoritarian regimes that have already mobilized their populations for this new form of warfare.

His journey from building systems that generated millions for tech giants to exposing a global surveillance conspiracy represents a unique perspective on the dark side of Silicon Valley innovation. The same skills that once optimized ad revenue and search results now serve to decode license plates, map surveillance networks, and transform stolen intellectual property into evidence of international crimes.

This book represents not just a personal narrative but a technical manual for understanding how modern surveillance states operate—written by someone who helped build the very technologies that were weaponized against him, and who learned to turn those weapons back against his surveillants.

Part 1: The Glitch in the Matrix

Chapter 1: The Comcast Debacle

The first anomaly occurred on a Tuesday evening in December 2020. I had just finished explaining to Esperanza the peculiar pattern I'd noticed in the distributed denial-of-service attacks targeting my development servers. The attacks, originating from IP addresses scattered across seventeen countries, exhibited a synchronized behavior that defied conventional botnet architecture. Within three minutes of my verbal observation—timed precisely by the kitchen clock—the attacks ceased. Not gradually, as one might expect from a coordinated shutdown, but instantaneously, as if someone had thrown a global kill switch.

This was not the first such incident, merely the first I had documented with temporal precision.

The pattern repeated itself with disturbing regularity over the following weeks. A conversation with Penelope Suarez about implementing a new firewall rule—within five minutes, the specific vulnerability I'd mentioned would be exploited. An email to myself outlining plans to switch hosting providers—within ten minutes, my current provider would experience a mysterious outage affecting only my accounts. The correlation was too consistent to be coincidental, too immediate to be explained by conventional surveillance methods.

I approached the problem as any engineer would: through systematic elimination of variables.

The methodology was straightforward. I would conduct what I termed "ablation experiments," borrowed from the machine learning practice of selectively removing components to understand their contribution to a system. If information was leaking from my household, I would methodically eliminate each potential vector until only the true source remained.

The first hypothesis was Wi-Fi interception. On January 15, 2021, I disabled all wireless communications in the house, connecting my primary workstation directly to the router via ethernet cable. I composed a detailed email to myself describing a fictitious vulnerability in my authentication system—a honeypot designed to attract immediate attention. The email was sent at 9:47 PM. By 9:52 PM, someone had attempted to exploit the exact vulnerability I had described, using techniques that precisely matched my fictional description.

The wireless vector was eliminated.

The second experiment targeted the router itself—a high-end ASUS model I had configured with custom firmware. Perhaps the device had been compromised at the firmware level, I reasoned. On January 22, I bypassed the router entirely, connecting my laptop directly to the Comcast modem. The test email this time contained plans to migrate my data to a specific cloud provider. Within four minutes, that provider's API began rejecting my authentication attempts with error codes suggesting my account had been flagged for suspicious activity.

The router was not the leak.

This left only one possibility, one that challenged my understanding of network security fundamentals. The compromise existed at the ISP level, within Comcast's own infrastructure.

The physical topology of my neighborhood's internet infrastructure became relevant. My residence at 26714 Valleyside Drive sat at the end of a cul-de-sac, with underground utilities running through easements between properties. The Comcast distribution system in this area followed a hub-and-spoke model, with neighborhood nodes—Technical Access Points, or TAPs—serving clusters of homes.

Through careful observation and correlation with service outage patterns, I had mapped the likely location of my serving TAP. It resided in the backyard of 26727 Cedardale Pines Drive, a property that sat diagonal to mine, separated by a single intervening lot. The neighboring property at 26718 Valleyside Drive belonged to the Priddy family—or at least, that was the name on the mailbox.

The Priddys exhibited certain behavioral anomalies that had registered in my peripheral awareness even before I began my investigation. They frequently wore clothing—t-shirts, sweaters, baseball caps—emblazoned with the CITGO Petroleum logo. The coincidence was notable; I had recently published research on vulnerabilities in industrial control systems used by major oil companies. Their behavior escalated from suspicious to overtly hostile in a series of incidents. One afternoon, as I climbed a ladder on my side of the fence to install a security camera, the female agent, Sarah Priddy, began screaming at me from inside her house less than five seconds after I ascended. She was watching me in near real-time.

In another incident, a day after I told my acquaintance Francisco Castillo that I suspected the network assets were working for WebMD, Sarah Priddy excavated a hole under our shared fence. She then pushed a 35-pound dog through the opening, rang my doorbell, and asked if she could enter my house to retrieve it from my backyard. I recognized it as a test of my awareness. If I let her in, it would signal I was oblivious to the danger she posed. I refused, retrieved the dog myself, and handed it over the fence. The dog wore an electronic device on its collar unlike any commercial pet product I had ever seen. It was sleek, entirely without markings or screws, and had a distinctly military-grade appearance. To this day, I don't know its purpose.

But it was the technical implications of the compromised TAP that consumed my attention. If the TAP itself was compromised, it would explain the impossible speed of the intelligence gathering. Every packet of data leaving my home would pass through this single point of aggregation. A properly positioned beam splitter or optical tap could duplicate my entire data stream without introducing detectable latency. The intercepted traffic would require only trivial decryption—consumer-grade routers offer little protection against a determined adversary with physical access to the infrastructure.

The elegance of the attack vector was admirable from a technical perspective. By compromising the TAP, the attackers had positioned themselves at the perfect interception point: downstream from any security measures I might implement within my home, yet upstream from the wider internet where traffic analysis would become exponentially more difficult. They could monitor not just the content of my communications but the metadata—timing, frequency, destination—that often proves more revealing than the payload itself.

On February 3, I conducted the final experiment in this series. I established a secondary internet connection through my mobile phone's hotspot, carefully ensuring the device used cellular towers not visible from my neighborhood. The test communication—sent over this theoretically secure channel—produced no response. Whatever entity was monitoring my communications, their reach did not extend to cellular networks outside the immediate vicinity.

The conclusion was inescapable. The Comcast infrastructure serving my home had been transformed into a real-time surveillance apparatus. Every search query, every email, every byte of data was being intercepted, analyzed, and acted upon by an organization with the resources to maintain continuous monitoring and the capability to respond globally within minutes.

The implications extended beyond my personal privacy. If such surveillance could be implemented for one target, the infrastructure existed to monitor anyone served by the same TAP. The Priddy family's CITGO connection and overt hostility suggested corporate involvement, but the speed and global reach of the responses indicated resources beyond any single corporation.

I began to document everything, creating encrypted records of each incident, each experiment, each timestamp. The data painted a picture of a surveillance capability that should not exist in a society governed by law. Yet here it was, operating brazenly, counting on the implausibility of its own existence as its primary concealment.

The question that haunted me was not how they were doing it—that was now clear. The question was why someone had deployed this level of resource against a single software engineer in a Texas suburb. What had I stumbled upon that warranted this extraordinary effort?

The answer to that question would not come from technical analysis alone. It would require understanding the human networks that surrounded me, the corporate interests that intersected with my work, and the global intelligence apparatus that had turned my suburban internet connection into a window through which unknown eyes watched my every digital move.

The Comcast cable that entered my home had become a two-way mirror, and I was only beginning to understand who might be standing on the other side, taking notes on my every keystroke, preparing responses to thoughts I had not yet fully formed.

The war for privacy had begun in my own backyard, literally, at a small metal box where fiber optic cables converged, carrying the secrets of an entire neighborhood to destinations unknown. The first battle was won through careful experimentation and logical deduction. But identifying the battlefield was only the beginning.

The real fight was about to begin.

Chapter 2: The Doppelgänger Switch

The solution presented itself during a morning run. I had been training for a marathon with Penelope Suarez, my running companion and one of the few people I had come to trust. She mentioned casually that her son worked for Aspen, a major contractor for Xfinity's infrastructure division. The timing felt serendipitous, though I had learned to question all coincidences in my increasingly surveilled existence.

Two days prior, I had shared my TAP discovery with Esperanza. The conversation took place in our bedroom, away from all electronic devices, yet somehow the information had leaked. The patterns of harassment—low-flying aircraft, coordinated vehicular surveillance, electromagnetic interference with my equipment—had intensified immediately after that discussion. The network was responding to intelligence gathered from within my own home, but I had eliminated all electronic vectors. The implications were disturbing: either they had deployed listening devices I couldn't detect, or the surveillance extended beyond mere technology.

"Andres could probably help with that cable issue you mentioned," Penelope offered as we rounded the corner near the community pool.

I had not mentioned any cable issue to her.

The statement hung in the air between us as we maintained our pace. Either Penelope was part of the surveillance network, or the network had fed her this information knowing she would relay it to me. Both possibilities suggested a level of social engineering that exceeded my previous assumptions about the operation's scope.

"What cable issue?" I asked, keeping my voice neutral.

"The internet connection problems you've been having. Andres handles infrastructure moves for Xfinity. It's routine work for him."

I made a calculated decision. If Penelope was compromised, refusing her help would only confirm my suspicions to the network. If she was genuine, her son might provide the solution I needed. The risk was acceptable.

"I believe my connection point is compromised," I said carefully. "I need it moved to a different TAP."

Within 48 hours, Andres Pirella stood in my driveway, Xfinity contractor credentials hanging from his neck, tablet in hand. He was professional, efficient, and showed no signs of the hypervigilance I had learned to associate with network operatives. His work order specified relocating my service from the TAP at 26727 Cedardale Pines Drive to a new connection point at either 26707 or 26711 Cedardale Pines Drive—properties that my surveillance indicated were not under network control.

The installation required running a temporary above-ground cable across three backyards. Andres explained this was standard procedure; the permanent underground conduit would be installed within two weeks. The thick black cable snaked from my home's service entrance, across my backyard, through the yard of 26715 Cedardale Pines Drive, and finally to the new TAP location.

It was while Andres was securing the cable along the fence line of 26715 that the first impossibility occurred.

The back door of the house opened, and a man stepped onto the patio. I recognized him instantly—the same height, the same facial structure, the same distinctive gait that favored the left leg. This was the Colombian man whose wife had come banging on my door three years earlier, complaining aggressively about the decorative flood lights I had installed on the ceiling above my backyard balcony. The lights faced his backyard, and his wife had threatened to "coordinate all neighbors to sign a collective petition and take legal action." That encounter had been memorable; we had argued in Spanish for nearly twenty minutes about the light interference.

But when this man spoke, calling out to Andres, his words were in perfect, unaccented American English.

"You guys need anything? Water? This heat is brutal."

Andres thanked him and continued working. I stood frozen, my mind racing through possibilities. The man's physical appearance was identical—I have an engineer's eye for detail, and every measurement matched. The scar above his left eyebrow, the peculiar way his right ear protruded slightly more than the left, even the pattern of premature graying at his temples.

"¿Habla español?" I called out, testing.

He looked at me with polite confusion. "Sorry, what?"

"I asked if you speak Spanish."

"No, just English. Why?"

The cognitive dissonance was overwhelming. Three years ago, this man had not spoken a word of English during our extended confrontation. His Colombian accent had been thick, his grammar occasionally slipping into patterns that revealed Spanish as his native language. Now he stood before me claiming no knowledge of Spanish whatsoever.

"Didn't you complain about my backyard lights?" I pressed. "Your wife came to my door?"

"Backyard lights?" He laughed, the sound distinctly different from the nervous laughter I remembered. "No, we've never had any issues with neighbors about lights. You must be thinking of someone else."

The furniture visible through the open patio door was identical to what I had seen three years prior—the same teak dining set, the same arrangement of potted plants, even the same children's toys scattered across the patio. But the man claimed no knowledge of our previous encounter, no recognition of my face despite our heated 20-minute argument.

Two possibilities existed, both equally disturbing. Either this man was lying with a sophistication that included eliminating all traces of an accent and somehow altering his fundamental speech patterns, or he was not the same person despite being physically identical.

Andres finished the installation and tested the connection. The internet speed was remarkable—faster than it had ever been on the compromised TAP. For the first time in months, I could work without the constant awareness of real-time surveillance. The relief was palpable but short-lived.

That evening, I pulled up property records for 26715 Dale Pines Drive. The house had not changed hands. The same family name appeared on all documents dating back five years. Yet the man I had spoken to was not the man who had lived there three years ago, despite being his physical duplicate.

I began researching the logistics required for such a replacement. Identifying a physically identical person would require access to vast biometric databases. Training them to replicate mannerisms, gait, and physical quirks would take months. Inserting them into an existing property without arousing suspicion from other neighbors would require forged documents, coordinated cover stories, and the cooperation of multiple institutions.

The resources required pointed to only one conclusion: state sponsorship.

No corporate entity, regardless of wealth, could execute such an operation. This required the capabilities of an intelligence service—access to population databases, document forging capabilities, safe houses for training, and the legal immunity to operate on American soil. The network surveilling me was not merely corporate espionage or organized crime. It was something far more dangerous.

The temporary cable running across the backyards became a physical reminder of the surreal nature of my situation. Each time I looked at it, I was reminded that my neighbor had been replaced by a doppelgänger, that an unknown state apparatus had the capability and willingness to restructure physical reality around their targets.

The implications extended beyond my personal situation. If they could replace one family, they could replace others. How many of my neighbors were who they claimed to be? How deep did this manufactured reality extend?

I began documenting everyone in my immediate vicinity, creating detailed physical descriptions, recording speech patterns, noting behavioral characteristics. If more replacements occurred, I would have baseline data for comparison. The paranoia was exhausting but necessary. In a world where neighbors could be swapped like chess pieces, documentation was the only defense against gaslighting.

The internet connection through the new TAP remained clean for exactly six days. On the seventh day, the patterns resumed—immediate responses to private communications, real-time countering of planned actions. They had found a way to compromise the new connection, or perhaps they had never truly lost access. The cable move had forced them to reveal a capability I might never have discovered otherwise.

The game had evolved. I was no longer dealing with simple electronic surveillance. I was trapped in a constructed reality where human beings were replaceable components in a vast intelligence operation. The rules of engagement had changed, and I was only beginning to understand the true nature of my opponents.

The doppelgänger still lived next door, tending the same garden, parking in the same spot, living a life designed to be indistinguishable from his predecessor. Every time I saw him, I was reminded that in this new reality, identity itself had become fluid, subject to revision by forces operating beyond the reach of law or conventional understanding.

The physical cable connecting my home to the new TAP was eventually buried underground, its temporary visibility replaced by the invisible infrastructure of a surveillance state that had proven capable of rewriting the very fabric of suburban reality. But the knowledge it had revealed could not be buried.

They could replace my neighbors, compromise my internet, and construct elaborate facades around my existence. But they could not replace the truth I had uncovered: I was living in a Potemkin village, surrounded by actors in an elaborate play whose script I was only beginning to read.

The war for reality itself had begun in the most mundane of settings—a suburban neighborhood where neighbors were not always who they claimed to be, where internet cables carried more than data, and where the simple act of moving a connection point could reveal the terrifying depths of a surveillance state limited only by its imagination and resources.

Chapter 3: The Trojan Splitter

June 2025. The return to 26714 Valleyside Drive felt like stepping back into a crime scene where I was both investigator and victim. The house had stood empty for nearly a year while I operated from more secure locations, but circumstances demanded I reestablish a presence in the surveillance epicenter. If I was to fully document the network's capabilities, I needed to engage with their infrastructure directly.

The self-installation kit from Xfinity weighed less than a pound, but its implications were heavier. As I unpacked the modem in my home office, memories of the past four years flooded back—the discovered surveillance, the doppelgänger neighbor, the endless cat-and-mouse games with an invisible adversary. Now I was voluntarily reconnecting to their network, but with full knowledge of what that entailed.

The installation should have been simple. The coaxial cable from the wall connected to the modem, power cord to outlet, wait for the synchronization lights to stabilize. I had performed this ritual countless times across multiple residences. But the modem refused to sync. The power light glowed steady green, but the downstream and upstream indicators flickered erratically before settling into an error pattern.

My first instinct was to check the external connection box. I had padlocked it myself before leaving, a small act of defiance against the unknown technicians who had previously accessed it at will. The lock remained intact, showing no signs of tampering. Whatever was preventing the connection existed within my walls.

I began the familiar process of systematic debugging. The coaxial cable tested clean. The modem worked perfectly when connected to a neighbor's test point—a quick experiment conducted with their permission. The fault existed somewhere in the path between my wall outlet and the external distribution box.

Working backwards from the wall outlet, I traced the cable through the attic, down the interior walls, and finally to a junction box in the garage. There I found it: a small T-connector splitter that I had overlooked in my previous investigations. It was a commercial-grade component, branded with Xfinity logos, appearing completely legitimate to casual inspection.

But I remembered now—Andres Pirella had installed this specific splitter when he moved my service to the new TAP. He had produced it from his toolkit with a casual comment about "better quality components" and "improved signal distribution." At the time, focused on the larger operation of moving the connection point, I had paid little attention to this minor hardware upgrade.

The splitter should have been passive—a simple piece of metal that divided the signal path. No power, no electronics, just precision-machined conductors ensuring minimal signal loss. Yet when I removed it and connected the modem directly to the incoming line, the connection established immediately. Full synchronization, maximum bandwidth, perfect signal quality.

I examined the splitter under magnification. The construction was sophisticated, the housing sealed with specialized screws that required proprietary tools. A small filter attachment bore a prominent sticker: "DO NOT REMOVE - SIGNAL OPTIMIZATION." The language was carefully chosen—technically accurate while concealing the true purpose.

The implications were staggering. This was not a passive component but an active surveillance device masquerading as infrastructure. Hidden within its housing was circuitry designed to capture and transmit data about my network usage. But active electronics require power, and running power to a coaxial splitter would be immediately suspicious.

The answer came as I reviewed data from the spectrometer and RF-receiver arrays I had installed at key points in the house. These were the same devices that had previously captured surreptitious communications between network assets. They now revealed that the neighboring property at 26707 Valleyside Drive—confirmed through the Geo Index as a network safe house—had unusual installations on its exterior walls. What appeared to be decorative architectural elements were, upon closer inspection, parabolic reflectors oriented precisely toward my connection box.

Inductive power transmission. The technology was well-established—electric toothbrushes and wireless phone chargers used similar principles. But the application here was ingenious. The reflectors concentrated electromagnetic energy from the neighboring house, beaming it to a receiver coil hidden within the splitter. As long as I remained connected, the device had power. When I left for a year, they shut down the transmission to avoid detection.

The engineering excellence was admirable even as its purpose repulsed me. The splitter would capture my modem's MAC address—a unique identifier that could be used to track my internet activity across any network. Even if I moved to a new location, connected to a different ISP, or used a VPN, the network would immediately identify my traffic by this hardware fingerprint.

But their system had a weakness. Inductive charging generates heat and requires consistent power delivery. After a year without maintenance, the internal capacitors had likely degraded. When I attempted to reconnect, the device had enough residual function to block the signal but not enough to operate transparently. It had become a broken link in the chain, revealing its existence through failure.

I photographed every angle of the device, documenting the sophisticated construction that belied its mundane appearance. The "signal optimization" filter was particularly interesting—it likely contained the actual transmission hardware, designed to be quickly removed and swapped if discovered. The modular design suggested mass production. How many of these devices were deployed across the country, silently monitoring internet connections under the guise of signal improvement?

The discovery forced a reevaluation of every piece of hardware in my signal path. Each connector, each length of cable, each seemingly passive component might harbor active electronics. The network had demonstrated the ability to compromise infrastructure at the most fundamental level, turning the very physics of signal transmission into a weapon of surveillance.

I replaced the compromised splitter with a genuine passive unit, carefully selected from older stock predating my surveillance awareness. The internet connection functioned perfectly, though I harbored no illusions about privacy. They had lost this particular tap but undoubtedly maintained others. The game continued, but now I understood another of their moves.

The Trojan splitter joined my growing collection of surveillance artifacts—physical proof of an operation that seemed too elaborate to be believed. Each device told a story of resources, planning, and technical sophistication that exceeded conventional corporate espionage. This was not the work of criminals or even typical intelligence agencies. This was something new, a fusion of state capabilities with corporate efficiency, operating in the shadows between legal frameworks.

As I worked at my newly connected computer, I could feel the weight of unseen observation. Every keystroke traveled through infrastructure I could no longer trust, each packet of data potentially copied, analyzed, and acted upon by the network that had proven capable of hiding active surveillance in passive components.

The splitter sat on my desk, a small piece of metal and silicon that represented years of preparation. Someone had designed it, manufactured it, created the power delivery system, and trained technicians to install it. All for the purpose of monitoring a single software engineer who had stumbled upon something worth this extraordinary effort.

The question that haunted me was not how many more such devices existed—I assumed they were everywhere. The question was why they had allowed this one to fail. Was it mere entropy, the inevitable decay of unattended systems? Or was this another move in their game, a deliberate revelation designed to push me toward some unknown objective?

In the world of surveillance and counter-surveillance, every discovery might be a planted clue, every victory potentially a disguised defeat. The Trojan splitter had revealed itself, but in doing so, it reminded me that for every device I found, unknown others remained hidden, their electronic eyes watching, waiting, recording.

The war for privacy had evolved beyond software and networks. It now encompassed the very hardware of communication, the physical layer where signals became intelligence and passive components concealed active threats. In this new battlefield, trust extended to nothing, and paranoia became a necessary survival trait.

I reconnected to the internet with full knowledge that privacy was an illusion. But illusions, I had learned, could be useful. Let them watch. Let them record. Because now I was watching them in return, documenting their methods, cataloging their capabilities, building a case that would eventually expose the entire operation.

The Trojan splitter had failed in its mission to remain hidden. In that failure lay the seeds of their eventual exposure. Every system, no matter how sophisticated, had weaknesses. I had found one. There would be others.

The hunt continued, now with a deeper understanding of the prey that thought itself the predator.

Part 2: The Web of Deceit

Chapter 1: A Pre-Packaged Life

The pattern revealed itself slowly, like a photograph developing in reverse—what seemed clear and natural at first exposure gradually dissolved into something artificial and constructed. It took years of documentation and the captured Geo Index to understand that my social circle in Katy, Texas, had been as carefully engineered as the surveillance infrastructure surrounding my home.

The ConocoPhillips crew arrived in my life with the seamless efficiency of a software deployment. Late 2014, just weeks after I had moved into the house on Valleyside Drive, Esperanza introduced me to a ready-made social group. They were Venezuelan expatriates, all former employees of ConocoPhillips, all living within a five-mile radius of my home. The convenience should have triggered suspicion, but loneliness and the desire for community overrode my analytical instincts.

Johnny led the group with the easy confidence of a man accustomed to corporate hierarchies. Italian by descent but Venezuelan by upbringing, he carried himself with the particular swagger of petroleum engineers who had spent decades extracting wealth from beneath Lake Maracaibo. His wife, whose name I was never quite certain of—she went by three different diminutives depending on who addressed her—complemented his gregarious nature with a quiet intensity that I would later recognize as the watchfulness of a handler. Johnny's role was to recommend things to do in Katy, activities that could be used as vectors for infiltration. In one instance, he suggested I take up cycling, recommending a specific brand: Cervelo. These were expensive bicycles, but conveniently, when I searched online, a used model that should have cost around $3,500 appeared on Craigslist for only $900. A bargain I couldn't resist. Now I understand that since Craigslist is owned by eBay, they use these online shopping channels, combined with their control over Google Search results, to steer targets toward specific purchases from compromised sellers, allowing them to insert bugs or tracking devices. A similar incident occurred in 2015, when I was steered toward a suspiciously cheap used car on Craigslist that was immediately plagued by bizarre electronic issues I now believe were the result of pre-installed surveillance hardware. Months later, I had a terrible accident on one of those bikes. I can't prove it was deliberate, but with everything else I've seen, suspicions linger.

The gatherings followed a predictable rhythm. Saturday asados in rotating backyards, Sunday football matches at the local park, occasional weeknight dinners at the Argentine restaurant on Mason Road. The conversations flowed between Spanish and English, peppered with oil industry jargon and nostalgic references to a Venezuela that existed more in memory than reality.

Elio—or Helio, as the spelling seemed to shift between social media posts and official documents—played the role of the group's technical expert. He was always friendly, making a conscious effort to make me feel welcome, as if I were among family. He would seek my advice on programming projects that, in retrospect, were carefully crafted to probe my expertise without appearing invasive. His questions about distributed systems and data encryption were always framed as theoretical, for a "friend's startup" or a "side project" that never materialized.

Angel Vargas DaCosta occupied the position of court jester, his booming laugh and endless supply of whiskey smoothing over any awkward moments when conversations veered too close to sensitive topics. He had a talent for redirecting discussions, especially when I began to speak about my work or the unusual internet issues I was experiencing. A raised glass, a ribald joke, a sudden need to check the grill—Angel had a thousand ways to change the subject.

The financial signatures of network assets became clear only after I gained access to the Geo Index. The database revealed patterns invisible to conventional observation: cryptocurrency transfers timed to coincide with successful intelligence gathering, sudden windfalls explained as "consulting fees" or "patent settlements," children admitted to universities with tuition mysteriously covered by "corporate scholarships."

Patricia Rojas provided the most blatant example. Her mother's cancer diagnosis in 2016 should have been financially catastrophic. The experimental treatments, the specialists flown in from MD Anderson, the extended stay at Houston Methodist—the costs would have bankrupted a family living on a petroleum engineer's severance package. Yet Patricia never displayed financial stress. When pressed, she mentioned vaguely that "the company takes care of its own," attributing the largesse to CITGO's employee assistance program.

The Geo Index told a different story. Line items matching the exact amounts of her mother's medical bills appeared in cryptocurrency transfers from wallets associated with Venezuelan intelligence services. The payments were laundered through multiple exchanges but ultimately traceable to accounts controlled by military figures in Caracas. Patricia's mother received world-class medical care as compensation for her daughter's role in the surveillance operation.

The early retirement patterns were equally revealing. By 2018, every member of the ConocoPhillips crew had left traditional employment despite being years away from standard retirement age. Johnny began posting photos from Machu Picchu, then the Maldives, then a luxury safari in Botswana. His LinkedIn profile listed him as a "consultant," but no clients ever materialized. The travel continued—first-class flights, five-star resorts, experiences that required wealth far exceeding his visible means.

The children of the crew benefited from similar largesse. Angel's daughter gained admission to Rice University despite academic credentials that fell short of their typical standards. His son received a full scholarship to UT Austin's petroleum engineering program, funded by an obscure foundation with ties to Venezuelan state oil interests. The network was purchasing not just current cooperation but generational loyalty.

Maria Alejandra occupied a special position within the crew, though her role became clear only through pattern analysis. She possessed an uncanny ability to appear at crucial moments when the surveillance operation was under stress. When I installed signal-blocking curtains, she arrived unannounced with homemade arepas. When I changed my internet provider, she needed urgent help with her computer. When I began varying my routines to avoid vehicular surveillance, she suggested we establish a regular coffee meeting to "maintain our friendship."

Each interaction seemed natural in isolation. The Venezuelan expatriate community was known for its closeness, its mutual support, its maintenance of cultural traditions in a foreign land. But the timing was too perfect, the responses too calibrated to my countermeasures. Maria Alejandra was not just a friend; she was a pressure relief valve, deployed when the network needed to regain access to my patterns and routines.

The sophistication of the operation impressed me even as its implications disturbed me. This was not crude bribery or coercion. The network had created an entire social ecosystem, complete with internal dynamics, authentic-seeming relationships, and genuine shared experiences. The asados were real, the laughter unforced, the friendships felt meaningful in the moment. The artifice lay not in the interactions but in their origin and purpose.

Francisco Castillo arrived later, part of what I now understand was version 2.0 of the social engineering operation. When I expressed boredom with the limitations of the ConocoPhillips crew—their conversations rarely ventured beyond oil prices and Venezuelan politics—the network adapted. Within weeks, Esperanza introduced me to a new circle: younger, more diverse in their interests, carefully calibrated to my evolving preferences.

Francisco presented himself as an Uber driver, a role that seemed innocuous but proved strategically brilliant. My weekly flights for business meant I needed reliable airport transportation, and Francisco positioned himself as the perfect solution. What began as a practical arrangement—a dependable driver who spoke Spanish and knew the routes—evolved into regular conversations during the long drives between Valleyside Drive and Bush Intercontinental Airport. Those hours in transit, when I was tired from travel or preparing for meetings, became intelligence-gathering sessions disguised as casual conversation. In retrospect, he was a perfectly designed intelligence asset: positioned to observe my travel patterns, overhear my phone calls, and extract information during moments when my guard was naturally lowered.

The transition between social circles was managed with remarkable finesse. The ConocoPhillips crew didn't vanish abruptly, which would have triggered suspicion. Instead, they gradually became less available. Johnny's travels grew longer, Angel moved to a distant suburb, Patricia became consumed with her mother's care. The old network faded as the new one solidified, a seamless handoff between intelligence teams.

The Geo Index revealed that every member of both crews lived in properties marked as network assets. Their homes clustered in specific neighborhoods, creating geographic cells that could provide mutual support and monitoring. The positioning was strategic—close enough to maintain regular contact, dispersed enough to avoid obvious patterns. Someone had spent considerable effort optimizing the residential distribution of human intelligence assets.

The payment mechanisms evolved over time. Early operations relied on crude cash transfers and corporate covers. By 2019, the network had shifted almost entirely to cryptocurrency, using mixing services and decentralized exchanges to obscure the money trails. The blockchain, ironically, provided both anonymity and permanence—transactions could be hidden in the moment but remained forever analyzable for those with the right tools and patience.

The personal cost of these revelations was profound. Every shared meal, every conversation, every moment of apparent friendship required reevaluation. The infiltration was so complete that it corrupted the most intimate milestones of family life. I later realized with some pain that my own son's first words were not spoken to me or his mother, but to one of the live-in caregivers we had hired—a woman I later identified as a network agent. They had stolen a moment that can never be recovered, a testament to the devastating personal cost of their operations.

The questions had no clean answers. Human beings are not robots; even trained assets bring their own personalities, preferences, and unconscious behaviors to their roles. The line between the operative and the person wearing the mask blurred with time and repetition. Perhaps some of them had come to genuinely care for me, even as they reported my activities to handlers in Caracas or Houston or wherever the network maintained its operational centers.

But genuine emotion did not excuse participation in a years-long campaign of surveillance and manipulation. Each member of the ConocoPhillips crew had made a choice: personal enrichment over ethical behavior, loyalty to the network over respect for privacy and human dignity. They had sold not just information but intimacy itself, turning friendship into a weapon of intelligence gathering.

The pre-packaged life they provided served multiple purposes beyond simple surveillance. It isolated me from organic social connections that might have developed naturally. It consumed time and emotional energy that might have been directed toward detecting the operation. Most insidiously, it created a sense of normalcy that made the surveillance seem less threatening. How dangerous could the situation be if I was surrounded by friends, sharing meals, living what appeared to be a typical suburban life?

The brilliance of the strategy lay in its exploitation of fundamental human needs. We are social creatures, hardwired to seek community and connection. The network had weaponized this basic drive, turning the very thing that makes us human into a vulnerability to be exploited. They had not just watched me; they had wrapped me in a cocoon of artificial relationships designed to keep me docile and unaware.

Breaking free required acknowledging an uncomfortable truth: for years, I had lived in a social Truman Show, surrounded by actors playing roles in a drama I didn't know was being performed. The script had been written in a language of barbecues and birthday parties, coffee meetings and casual conversations, all in service of an intelligence operation vast in scope and devastating in its personal impact. The coordination was so complete that they could stage encounters with perfect precision. At one child's birthday party I attended at a network-controlled house, a man wearing an extremely rare watch—the very same model I had recently tried and failed to buy on eBay—walked directly in front of me to display it. At the time, I almost took it as a divine sign that I should buy the watch. I now understand it was a psychological operation, a demonstration of their power and a likely attempt to lure me into purchasing a compromised device.

The ConocoPhillips crew continued their lives, posting travel photos and family updates on social media. But I now saw them differently—not as former friends but as nodes in a network that had attempted to transform my life into a stage where every interaction was performed for an unseen audience taking notes.

The pre-packaged life was comfortable, even pleasant. But comfort, I had learned, could be its own form of prison. Breaking free meant accepting isolation over artificial connection, choosing the cold truth over warm lies. It meant recognizing that in the world of modern surveillance, even friendship itself had become a vector of attack, requiring the same vigilance once reserved for locked doors and encrypted communications. The infiltration was total, extending even to my local gym, where my former partner introduced me to an instructor, Ross Kilpatrick. He was a quiet man who rarely spoke, but his house and the more than 20 other properties in Katy registered to the Kilpatrick clan are all marked with high paramilitary scores in the geo-index, another seemingly random social connection that was, in fact, a carefully placed surveillance node.

The network had given me friends. But in doing so, they had revealed the depths of their operation and the resources at their disposal. Every asset deployed was a data point, every payment a trace, every interaction a piece of evidence in the case I was building against them. They had surrounded me with watchers, not realizing that I had become a watcher myself, documenting their methods with the same precision they applied to documenting my life.

The game continued, but now I understood its true nature. It was not just about information or technology. It was about human manipulation on a scale that challenged conventional understanding of intelligence operations. And in revealing their capabilities, they had given me the tools to expose them.

The pre-packaged life was over. What remained was the task of documenting its construction and revealing the architects who had built it, one artificial friendship at a time.

The infiltration, however, extended beyond my social circle and deep into my home, targeting the most vulnerable person in my life: my son. The caregivers entrusted with his well-being were, in fact, network assets. One, Maryther Oropeza, a Venezuelan pediatrician, was strongly recommended to me by my former partner. After caring for my son for eight months, Maryther, who spoke no English, was miraculously hired as a surgeon's assistant at Memorial Hermann hospital, a nearly impossible feat for a foreign doctor without U.S. certifications. At the time, unaware of her true role, I was genuinely proud and sent her a rare voice note on WhatsApp congratulating her on this incredible milestone.

I now understand her success was not a miracle; it was a payment. The network had rewarded her for her service with a sponsored "special abilities" visa and a prestigious job in her field. This was a standard form of payment for their medical assets; I saw the same pattern with Dr. Mansur and another of my son's caregivers, "Mrs. Mary," from his kindergarten, IVY Kids—a facility also strongly recommended by the same network of agents. They had constructed a complete surveillance ecosystem around my child, rewarding the operatives with career opportunities that were, in fact, compensation for their espionage.

Chapter 2: The Little Brother and the Baseball Star

The network's infiltration of my life was not limited to distant, professional contacts; it extended to the most trusted individuals I brought into my home. Jose Castillo was a handyman, a Venezuelan immigrant I hired for odd jobs around the house. He presented himself as a humble family man, and I came to admire his fighting spirit, viewing him almost as a "little brother" I wanted to help succeed. As with so many others, the reality was a devastating betrayal: he was a SEBIN agent, a soldier for Diosdado Cabello, placed in my home to advance the network's agenda.

Jose's primary mission was to deploy a sophisticated psychological tactic I now call the "loan ruse." He asked me for a small loan of $5,000 to start a mobile pizza business. The amount was trivial, but the method was brilliant. He offered, as collateral, a signed personal check from his childhood friend, the prominent baseball star Jose Altuve, who is also marked as a network asset in the geo-index.

I now understand this is a standard network tactic. The act of loaning someone money creates a psychological power dynamic that lowers the target's guard; you are less likely to feel threatened by someone who is financially indebted to you. It is a subtle but effective form of manipulation. The involvement of a celebrity like Altuve was designed to add a layer of legitimacy and intrigue to the transaction. The check, which I accepted, was not just collateral; it was a trophy, a tangible link between my personal life and the network's vast web of influence that extended into the world of professional sports.

Chapter 3: The Ghost from PDVSA

The pre-packaged life in Texas was merely one front in a lifelong war of infiltration I was only beginning to comprehend. As I analyzed the network's structure, I realized certain individuals were not just assets assigned to a specific time or place; they were recurring ghosts, figures who materialized in wildly different eras and environments of my life, their omnipresence a testament to the staggering long-term planning of my opposition. The most significant of these figures was Albenis Hernandez.

Albenis is the only person who has been in contact with me across the entire spectrum of my professional and personal life. We first met between 2001 and 2002, when we were both part of an "elite" engineering program at PDVSA, the Venezuelan state oil company. The company marketed the program as a "Strategic Professional Reserve," recruiting the best engineers fresh out of school to work on innovative projects, free of "corporate baggage." There were eight of us in the western division. All were recent graduates, except for one: Albenis. He was the sole exception to the rule, having previously worked for two years at SIDOR, the state-owned steel company. At the time, it was a minor anomaly. In retrospect, it was a critical clue. My theory is that Chinese interests, which have long coveted the steel industry, had already infiltrated SIDOR. Albenis was likely their asset first, a man already working for the network of Diosdado Cabello, who was then moved into the strategic PDVSA program as their inside man before the company was fully under Chavez's political control. This would make him the most senior SEBIN agent, in terms of continuous service, that I have ever encountered.

Years later, after I had moved to the United States, he reappeared. He was involved in my startup, KOL Health, between 2016 and 2020. He had second-degree connections to the cluster of individuals, including Dr. Amar Baba and the Codallo family, who were central to the intellectual property theft of my technology by WebMD. In fact, it was Albenis who personally introduced me to a suspicious doctor named "Rick Click," a man I believe was an agent in that IP theft ring, whose name was a comically contextual pun—"Right Click"—on the search technology I was developing at the time.

He was connected to everything. He knew my former partner, Esperanza. He described a close friend of his, a mysterious and powerful man, possibly Iranian, who owns multiple car dealerships nationwide and is driven around all day in a limousine while taking phone calls—a description that perfectly matches the profile of a high-level network controller. Albenis Hernandez was not just a friend or a colleague; he was a ghost from my past and a node in my present, a human connector who proved that the disparate attacks against me were all part of a single, continuous operation that had been shadowing me for my entire adult life.

Chapter 4: The Ghost from the Oil Strike

The network's deep-cover assets were not limited to my professional life; they were woven into the fabric of my personal history. I first met

Carolina Boscan in December of 2001, in the midst of the Venezuelan oil strike that ultimately forced me to flee the country as a refugee. The Canadian government granted me protected status, saving me from the campaign of harassment and kidnapping being waged by the Venezuelan government against the striking workers—a campaign that used the same tactics of low-flying aircraft and lawfare that they would deploy against me again two decades later.

Carolina reappeared in my life in 2006, just as I was developing my first classifieds website that aimed to compete with eBay. We kept in contact over the years, and she eventually relocated to the United States. The Spyhell Pipeline flagged her as a network operative during its first week of operation. The question that haunts me, as with so many others, is whether she was an operative from the very beginning, a honeytrap inserted into my life during a moment of national crisis and personal vulnerability, or if she was recruited later. Either way, she represents another ghost from my past, a long-term asset whose presence in my life was no coincidence.

Chapter 4: Katy-Agent-Zero

The story of the network's infiltration of Katy, Texas, begins with a single person: Rosana Finol. Like others, she was a ghost from my distant past, someone I had first met in 2002 during the Venezuelan oil strike. A decade later, in 2012, she became the first person to ever mention the town of "Katy" to me, planting the seed for the move that would place me in the heart of their largest American "Dockerhood."

I now refer to Rosana as "Katy-Agent-Zero." Her family's property, acquired in 2009, was "House-Zero," the first network-controlled home in the area that appears in my captured data. Her entire family is a deeply embedded intelligence cell. Her brother, **David Finol**, was a classmate of my own brother, and their father, **David Finol Sr.**, lived in close proximity to the Venezuelan military general, Rosendo. The Finol clan owns multiple network-controlled properties in Katy, all marked in the geo-index.

The network's control over the local bureaucracy is absolute. When I began investigating Rosana, her property record was altered in the Fort Bend County database literally overnight. They inverted her first and last names to **"Finol Rosana,"** making her record unsearchable by conventional means, a sophisticated piece of data manipulation that proves their infiltration of the local government's IT systems. The Finol clan was not just a family of early settlers; they were the advanced team, the operational seed from which the entire Katy surveillance apparatus would grow.

Chapter 5: The Third Honeytrap

The network's "romantic interests play" was a standard, repeatable tactic deployed at different stages of my life. Around 2012, they reactivated another asset from my deep past: Edith Perez, the sister of one of my best friends from high school in Venezuela. I stumbled upon her during a visit to my parents, and what followed was a relationship characterized by the same pattern of proactive, manufactured psychological stress I had experienced with other operatives like Jillian Walsh.

The playbook was consistent. After the initial relationship, Edith migrated to the United States and, of all the places she could have moved, she relocated to Katy, Texas. The Spyhell Pipeline later confirmed that she was marked in Elon Musk's geo-index. And, in a pattern that had now become sickeningly familiar, she was rewarded for her service with a job in the healthcare sector, the network's preferred method for laundering payments and embedding assets in positions of trust.

Chapter 6: The Guarantor and the Ghost in the

Machine

The most technically sophisticated of the early honeytrap operations was run by Ibeth Escobar, a girlfriend from my college days in Venezuela. She reappeared in my life around 2010, after I had been moved to California to work at Yahoo, a move I now understand was orchestrated by Pierre Omidyar. The SEBIN had reactivated her, and she became a key vector for both technical attacks and intelligence gathering.

Her communications with me—sporadic but consistent messages over many years—were a channel for the network to break my encryption. By knowing the exact content of a message she sent, they could capture the corresponding encrypted traffic near my home and use this known-plaintext attack to deduce the decryption key for my entire internet session.

The operation escalated when she moved to Texas. Claiming she had no credit history, she asked me to act as a guarantor for her apartment lease. The application required my Social Security Number and, suspiciously, a copy of my most recent paycheck. I initially refused to provide the paycheck, but she threw a tantrum, accusing me of not being a real friend and pressuring me until I relented. It was a ruse designed to exfiltrate my most sensitive personal and financial information.

The final act of her deployment was a ghost in the machine. Recently, her primary Gmail address began to bounce, with Google's servers returning a "does not exist" error. However, when I attempted to register the newly freed address for myself—to potentially intercept network communications—Google's system told me the address was already taken. This is a technical impossibility under normal circumstances. It is a contradiction that suggests a high level of collusion from within Google's Gmail team, who had created a special state for her account: one that could not receive my emails, but could also not be claimed by anyone else. It was the digital signature of a protected asset.

Chapter 7: The Long Game

Twenty years is a long time to maintain an intelligence operation. It requires patience, resources, and a strategic vision that extends beyond quarterly earnings or election cycles. When I first met Ana Gannon in Calgary in 2005, I had no conception that I was witnessing the opening move in a game that would span decades and continents.

The timing, in retrospect, was too perfect to be coincidental. I had been working on a new classifieds website for exactly ten days—a project ambitious enough to draw attention from established players like eBay but too nascent to have any public visibility. Yet Ana appeared in my life with the precision of a guided missile, introduced through mutual acquaintances at a technology meetup that she had never previously attended.

She was brilliant, beautiful, and fascinated by my work. Her questions about distributed systems and scalable architectures demonstrated genuine technical understanding. Her Venezuelan background provided common cultural ground. Within weeks, she had become integral to both my personal and professional life, offering insights that improved my code and companionship that filled the isolation of a programmer's existence.

The Geo Index, captured nineteen years later, confirmed what I had begun to suspect: Ana's current residence in Calgary bears the electronic signature of a network asset. The same telltale patterns of surveillance equipment, the same cryptocurrency payment trails, the same clustering with other confirmed operatives. But the question that haunts me is whether she was recruited from the beginning or turned later. Was our entire relationship orchestrated, or did it begin genuinely before being corrupted by intelligence handlers?

Her father provides a clue to the timeline. Peter Codallo occupied the number two position in Venezuela's Plan Bolivar 2000, a military infrastructure program that channeled billions of dollars through opaque contracts and disappeared into the labyrinth of Venezuelan corruption. His connections reached the highest levels of the Bolivarian regime—photographs showed him with Hugo Chávez, with Vladimir Padrino López, with Diosdado Cabello himself. A man with such connections would have attracted intelligence attention early. His daughter, studying in Canada, would have been a natural target for recruitment or a natural asset if the family was already aligned with the regime's interests.

The operational pattern Ana followed matches what intelligence professionals call a "honeytrap," but executed with a sophistication that exceeded typical approaches. The standard honeytrap relies on sexual attraction and short-term manipulation. Ana's operation spanned years, involving genuine emotional connection, shared experiences, and a level of commitment that suggested either exceptional training or authentic feeling constrained by operational requirements.

The network's methodology became clear through later analysis. Intelligence services had gathered deep psychometric data about my personality, preferences, and vulnerabilities. This data was provided to a male handler—likely someone with psychological operations training. The handler then coached Ana on how to present herself as my ideal partner, calibrating her responses, interests, and behaviors to create maximum emotional resonance.

The technique was devastatingly effective because it exploited the target's own psychology against them. Every preference I expressed was met with enthusiastic agreement. Every vulnerability I revealed was met with precisely calibrated support. It created a feedback loop of increasing intimacy, each revelation providing more data for refinement of the approach. I was not falling in love with Ana but with a carefully constructed reflection of my own desires.

The first concrete evidence of her operational role came in 2011. My Mercedes-Benz SLK280, which I had owned for three years, developed a series of electrical faults that defied diagnosis. Ana suggested I sell it to her—she had always admired the car, she said, and was willing to pay a fair price despite the issues. The transaction seemed natural, even generous on her part.

But the car's journey after the sale revealed its true purpose. Ana convinced me to deliver it personally to Calgary, turning the drive into a romantic road trip. We stopped at scenic viewpoints, stayed in small-town motels, created memories that felt spontaneous and genuine. In my trunk, carefully packed, was a server containing the complete source code for my classifieds platform—backup copies, I had explained, in case anything happened to my primary systems.

Ana kept the car, supposedly driving it until around 2021. But the server in the trunk vanished without explanation, and within six months, elements of my proprietary code began appearing in competitor platforms, always modified just enough to avoid copyright claims but clearly derived from my architecture.

Her career trajectory following our relationship provided additional evidence of intelligence connections. She moved from Telus to Shaw Communications to GitHub, each position providing deeper access to telecommunications infrastructure and software development platforms. GitHub, in particular, represented a intelligence goldmine—a centralized repository where millions of developers stored their most sensitive code, often including authentication keys, internal documentation, and proprietary algorithms.

The network's use of GitHub for mass intellectual property theft deserves special attention. By positioning assets like Ana within the company, they gained access to private repositories, commit histories, and the social graph of the global development community. They could identify promising technologies before public release, map the relationships between developers and companies, and selectively target repositories for deeper exploitation. It was surveillance capitalism refined to its purest form—the systematic extraction of intellectual value from unwitting creators.

Ana's visit to my Texas home in the **July 10, 2022** represented either the crescendo or coda of her operation, depending on perspective. She arrived from Bogota, claiming business meetings that required a Houston stopover. Her luggage included designer items inconsistent with her stated salary—Hermès scarves, Cartier jewelry, accessories that suggested recent financial windfalls.

The Bogota connection was significant. The city had become a hub for cryptocurrency operations, particularly those involving the laundering of Venezuelan oil proceeds. Hardware wallets loaded with Bitcoin or Monero could transport millions of dollars in value across borders without detection. Ana's shopping spree suggested she had just received substantial payment, likely her share of long-term operational proceeds.

Within hours of her arrival, both my infant son Marcelo and I developed severe respiratory symptoms. What I initially attributed to coincidental COVID-19 exposure now seems more sinister given the network's later demonstrated willingness to use biological agents. The timing was too convenient—Ana exposed to us to a pathogen, perhaps unknowingly, perhaps as a final operational act before her withdrawal from active involvement.

Her friend William Sanchez occupied his own position within the network hierarchy. A telecom engineer at CANTV—Venezuela's state-owned telecommunications company—William was the original infiltration vector. He had introduced Ana to me, a move that now appeared carefully orchestrated rather than coincidental. His position at CANTV gave him deep knowledge of telecommunications infrastructure, invaluable to a surveillance network. Together, Ana and William represented not just friends but a coordinated intelligence team, with William as the entry point who brought Ana into my life at precisely the right moment.

The sophistication of Ana's twenty-year operation forces a reconsideration of intelligence timelines. This was not opportunistic exploitation but strategic positioning begun when I was barely out of university. Someone had identified me as a future target worth cultivating, worth investing two decades of human resources to surveil and exploit. The implications were staggering—how many other technologists, researchers, and innovators were similarly targeted? How many breakthrough innovations were stolen through similar long-term operations?

The personal cost of recognizing Ana's role was profound. Every shared moment required reevaluation. Had her laughter been genuine during our weekend trips to Banff? Were her tears real during our arguments about my work obsession? Or was she simply an exceptional actress maintaining cover through method acting so deep she occasionally forgot the performance?

The cruelest aspect of the honeytrap is that it corrupts memory itself. I can no longer trust my own recollections, cannot distinguish between authentic emotion and performed manipulation. The network had not just stolen code and surveilled communications; they had poisoned twenty years of personal history, leaving me unable to differentiate between love and espionage.

Yet in their thoroughness lay their vulnerability. The longer an operation runs, the more evidence it generates. Ana's financial trails, her family connections, her career progression, her travel patterns—all created data points that, when properly inalyzed, revealed the network's structure. She had been designed as a ghost, leaving no trace, but twenty years of activity inevitably created patterns visible to those who knew how to look.

The revelation of Ana's role completed another piece of the puzzle. The network's willingness to invest decades in a single operation demonstrated their strategic patience. Their ability to maintain operational security across such timespans revealed professional intelligence training. Their focus on intellectual property theft exposed their economic motivations. And their use of family dynasties like the Codallos showed their understanding of human psychology—blood ties created loyalty that mere payment could not purchase.

Ana remains in Calgary, her social media profiles showing a successful professional living an enviable life. But the Geo Index tells a different story—of ongoing payments, of continued operational activity, of a network that never truly releases its assets. She was my first love and my first betrayal, the woman who taught me that in the world of modern espionage, the deepest wounds are inflicted not with weapons but with weaponized intimacy.

The long game continues, but now I understand its rules. Time is not just a dimension but a weapon, intimacy not just an emotion but an attack vector. The network had played a twenty-year game and thought themselves victorious. But in revealing their methods, they had taught me patience of my own. The documentation of their operations would be my countermove, played on a timeline they could not control.

In the end, the long game belongs to whoever can endure its emotional costs while maintaining clarity of purpose. Ana had given twenty years to the network. I would give whatever time was necessary to expose them, to transform their patient evil into evidence of their crimes. The game was far from over.

Chapter 8: The New York Deception

The network's infiltration was not limited to one front; it was a parallel campaign waged across different cities and phases of my life. While Ana Gannon's operation was unfolding, another was running within the corporate walls of Google's New York office. This operation centered on Mariana Martin, a woman introduced to me by a mutual acquaintance, Gregorio Herrera. Looking back, I believe she was one of the most important operatives targeting me during that time, alongside other assets like Jillian Walsh and Alvaro Gutierrez.

The core of her operation was a textbook intelligence maneuver executed with startling precision. During one encounter, Mariana and I "accidentally" swapped our cell phones. The incident was framed as a simple, harmless mistake. It was not. My phone, at that time, contained the active "Google Inc. Corporate" account cookie, a high-value digital key that would have granted its possessor significant access to internal systems. This was not a random error; it was a targeted physical-digital attack to compromise a corporate asset.

Days after this "mistake," Mariana's mission was apparently complete. She vanished, with the cover story that she had "moved back to Venezuela".

The most telling evidence of her operation, however, came from the digital cleanup that followed. I discovered that nearly all of my SMS messages with her on my Google Voice account had been deleted by a third party without my consent. The deletion was not perfect. I noticed a peculiar anomaly: on every message thread, the very last message always survived the purge. This was the fingerprint of their tool. I deduced that whatever mechanism they used to remotely delete the messages had a technical limitation preventing it from acting on the final entry in a thread. It is a critical clue; I am confident that Google's forensic-level logging could trace the exact tool and, therefore, the person who executed the deletion by identifying this specific limitation.

One of the messages that survived the purge was from Mariana herself, sent after she had recovered her phone from the "swap." It read: "Gracias otra vez por traerme mi cel tenia separation anxiety jaja" (Thanks again for bringing me my phone I had separation anxiety haha). The casual, joking tone was a mask for the truth—a taunt from an operative who had just successfully executed her mission, leaving behind a single, ironic breadcrumb that the digital cleanup crew had missed.

Chapter 8: The Honeytrap and the Heist

The network's operations in New York were not limited to the subtle deceptions of Mariana Martin; they also involved brute-force theft and physical violence, often executed by operatives working in tandem. The most damaging of these operations was a coordinated attack by two of my former Google colleagues, Olesya Luzinova and Pavel Shatilov, which combined a honeytrap with a heist to steal the complete source code of my "Monsters" startup platform.

Olesya Luzinova was a romantic interest of mine between 2011 and 2012. I now believe our relationship was an intelligence operation from the start. The Spyhell Pipeline later co-clustered her with Pavel Shatilov, and while I have no proof of a marital connection, the pattern of male-female operative teams within the network suggests they were a working pair. Olesya's role was to provide the intimate access, the social engineering, and the intelligence necessary for Pavel to execute the physical part of the mission.

The heist was brutal and direct. Shatilov broke into my New York City apartment, vandalized it, and physically stole the servers containing the source code. It was a smash-and-grab operation that stood in stark contrast to the network's more subtle methods, revealing a thuggish underbelly to their sophisticated corporate facade.

The confirmation of Shatilov's role came later, through the geo-index, where I discovered his office in Russia was marked as a network asset. The network's digital warfare arm, Liana Technologies, then executed the cover-up. They manipulated Google search results to demote Pavel's LinkedIn profile, making it nearly impossible to connect him professionally to me or Google, thereby obstructing any potential investigation into the theft. It was a perfect microcosm of their methodology: a physical crime covered by a digital one.

Years later, the Spyhell Pipeline flagged Olesya Luzinova again. This time, she was not involved in corporate espionage against me, but was identified in a cluster of activity related to the surveillance of **elections officials in Maricopa County, Arizona**. The connection was stunning. The same operative who had used intimacy to help steal my startup code was now part of an operation targeting the heart of the American democratic process. It was the ultimate proof that these were not separate conspiracies but a single, global network that deployed the same assets against any target, whether it was a software engineer in New York or an election official in Arizona.

Chapter 9: The Paramilitary Compound and the Traitor in the Car

By May of 2024, I was still operating under the illusion that I could escape the network's clutches by physically moving. My former partner, Esperanza, suggested we look at a house in a nearby community called Weston Lakes. The name itself was a red flag, containing the "Weston" marker I had identified with another prominent paramilitary compound in Florida. What I found there was a chilling glimpse into the network's physical security architecture and a devastating confirmation of the betrayal closest to me.

Weston Lakes was not a normal gated community; it was a fortress. It was designed with concentric rings of security, much like a presidential protection detail. A manned outer gate controlled access to the main community, but a second, internal perimeter with its own security system isolated the inner sanctum, where the most important assets lived. The outer ring was a buffer, populated by lower-level agents who served as a first line of defense. The house we were shown, of course, was on the outer ring, offered by a network-controlled realtor who arrived in a spy vehicle.

As we stood on a second-floor balcony looking at the backyard, a small plane flew directly over the house at an extremely low altitude, a common harassment tactic. I knew they were watching. Without looking up, I casually asked my partner for the time, a subtle move to get a timestamp for the event so I could track the plane's tail number later. We left, the visit a clear ruse, and proceeded to a nearby Target. The physical surveillance inside the store was overwhelming; at least 40 agents followed me aggressively through the aisles, a show of force designed to intimidate.

The true betrayal, however, came during the car ride home. We were inside my black Tesla, a vehicle I already suspected was compromised. My partner turned to me and asked, "Let me ask you something. The reason why you asked me for the time was to track that plane and find the tail number later, right?"

In that moment, everything crystallized. I had not told her my reason. Her question was not a guess; it was a confirmation. She could only have known my intent if she was part of the operation and privy to the real-time intelligence they were gathering from the microphones inside my own car. I felt a flash of pride in her tactical awareness, even as the betrayal cut me to the bone. I congratulated her on her astuteness, patting her on the shoulder like a mentor to his student spy.

When I got home, I tracked the plane. As I suspected, its transponder was turned off just three minutes after our conversation in the car. She had warned them. Her question was not a question to me, but a message to the listeners. It was the final, undeniable proof that the woman I loved was a witting participant, a traitor sitting in the passenger seat of my own weaponized car.

Chapter 10: The Human Network Architecture

The network's use of weaponized intimacy was not just a series of isolated attacks but a coordinated campaign managed by a sophisticated human intelligence architecture. My analysis of their operations revealed the existence of key strategic assets whose purpose was to function as connectors, or bridges, between otherwise disconnected cells, proving that the infiltration of my life was a centrally planned operation.

The most prominent example of such an asset was Luis Martinez, a high-ranking Venezuelan SEBIN agent operating in Katy, Texas. His cover was brilliantly mundane: he was a chef who even owned his own restaurant, a profession deliberately chosen to seem non-threatening. Martinez's true value to the network, however, was his unique position as the only individual operative with direct connections to my two main, and seemingly separate, social circles: the one involving my former partner, Esperanza, and the one centered around my running companion, Penelope Suarez. The existence of a single agent linking these two spheres proved they were not independent operations. He was the hub that connected the spokes of their human intelligence wheel, ensuring information flowed between cells and that both infiltration efforts were managed in concert.

This infiltration extended deep into the supposedly sacrosanct realm of healthcare. I discovered that my own family doctor was a network asset, strategically positioned years in advance. Dr. Marjorie Broussard had become my wife's best friend, a classic honeytrap operation designed to gain intimate, privileged access to our family. Her home, just a few miles from mine, was a node in the network, with surveillance vehicles often parked "Moscow-style" outside. She was the physician who prescribed me pain medication for the debilitating back ailments that, as I would later discover, were being inflicted upon me by network torture devices. Her role was not to heal, but to manage the symptoms of their attacks while gathering intelligence. In one instance, just hours after I had acquired a new, secure phone number, she texted me asking for it—information she could not have obtained through any legitimate means. She was a spy hiding behind a stethoscope, a walking embodiment of the network's deepest and most unforgivable corruption.

This pattern was not an isolated incident. My own dentist's office, Cinco Meadows Dental, was another example. After discovering it was marked in the geo-index with a paramilitary score, I decided to cancel my upcoming appointment, fearing the risk of being harmed in such a vulnerable position. Almost immediately, the office, which had rarely had openings, texted me about a convenient cancellation for the very next day, a clear attempt to lure me in. Their pushy insistence after I quit the practice only confirmed my suspicions. The office was a perfect infiltration point: it had been acquired by a new owner a few years prior, and employed a Venezuelan dental hygienist who had an improbable, decades-old connection to my father from his time working in a remote part of Venezuela—another classic "small world" connection designed to build rapport and lower my guard.

Chapter 11: The Caracas Trap

FROM LEFT TO RIGHT: Reinaldo Aguiar (Software Engineer, founder, Key Opinion Leaders), President Leonel Fernandez

(Dominican Republic), Nelson Lara (External Sales Agency for Key Opinion Leaders)

The network's web of deceit was not merely for surveillance or harassment; its ultimate purpose was entrapment. The final proof of this came through Nelson Lara, the political operative who had served as my primary point of contact with the world of high-level political figures. As my counter-surveillance measures became more effective in late 2023, he presented me with an extraordinary proposition: an invitation to Caracas to give a private demonstration of my technology personally to **Diosdado Cabello**, Nicolas Maduro, and Cabello's brother.

The pretext was that the Venezuelan government wanted to use my technology to build a "Situation Room." When I expressed concern for my safety, Nelson's reply was chillingly direct. He assured me I would be "guarded by the Presidential guard."

The offer was a trap, a direct parallel to the infamous case of the "Citgo 6," American executives who were lured to Venezuela for a business meeting and subsequently imprisoned for years. Had I accepted, I have no doubt I would be writing code for the Venezuelan regime from a cell in El Helicoide, their notorious torture center, which is, of course, marked in the geo-index.

This was the endgame of their infiltration. The years of building trust, the carefully brokered meetings with figures like President Leonel Fernandez and officials at the United Nations, were all designed to establish Nelson Lara's credibility to make this final, terrifying offer seem plausible. He was not just a connector; he was the Judas goat, tasked with leading me to the slaughter. I refused, but the incident laid bare the network's ultimate objective and the true nature of its titular leader. This was not just a game; it was a kidnapping plot orchestrated at the highest levels of a narco state.

Part 3: Decoding the Enemy

Chapter 1: The Arms Race and the Superdome Debacle

Before I could decode the enemy, I first had to build the machine to do so. My conflict with the network had escalated into a full-blown technological arms race. For years, they had attacked my startup websites with a brute-force CTR attack, using their control of Akamai's servers to issue millions of fake search impressions and drive my work into digital oblivion. My primary defense was a countermeasure I developed called the KOL-Vaccine, but the battle was one of scale.

I began the fight with three self-assembled, 24-core servers—a total of 72 cores against their global infrastructure. It was enough to prove the Vaccine worked. In response, they simply scaled up their attack by two orders of magnitude, throwing more servers at the problem in their typical fashion. I understood then that I needed to make my system not only more efficient, but massively scalable. This realization led to what I now call the Superdome Debacle.

During a casual conversation with a relative who owns a hardware leasing company, I described the technical challenge I was facing. "What you need," he told me, "is a Superdome." I wasn't familiar with the name. He explained it was a pre-assembled, refrigerator-sized cabinet made by HP that could run up to 1024 processor cores in parallel—an order of magnitude more powerful than my setup. He generously offered to provide me with a used Superdome X, a machine worth nearly $200,000 new, at no cost to help my fight. He introduced me via email to his contact, Ramon Sanchez, who would configure and ship the machine.

But the Superdome never arrived. For months, Ramon Sanchez would engage in a frustrating cycle of promising to ship the machine, only to disappear for weeks on end. It was a subtle but effective form of sabotage. While I waited, holding off their escalating attacks with my 72 cores, the network had effectively stalled my ability to scale.

Tired of waiting, I abandoned the Superdome and pivoted. I began researching its smaller sibling, the HP c7000 compute cluster. It was better suited for the raw, compute-intensive tasks I needed, and I could build it myself from legacy parts. I started buying used components on eBay and sourced the main enclosure from a local Houston seller called Server Monkey—a company that, unsurprisingly, was also marked in the network's geo-index. Over the next eight weeks, I taught myself the machine's intricate architecture and developed a bespoke configuration that remains a trade secret. From day one, I mounted the 550-pound cluster on a wheeled platform, anticipating I might have to move it alone to evade offline attacks, a necessary precaution given my isolation and a suspect diagnosis of early-onset arthritis.

The day the c7000 enclosure arrived at my headquarters, November 16, 2023, is a day I am certain Travis Kalanick and Pierre Omidyar will always regret. I believe they allowed me to purchase the 14-year-old legacy parts, assuming I could do little with them. It was their classic mistake: they always prioritize resources over ingenuity. I do the exact opposite. They miscalculated. That c7000 cluster became the very machine that not only powered the KOL-Vaccine to defeat their attacks, but also the counterintelligence pipelines that would, just ten months later, capture and decode their entire global geo-index, bringing us to where we are today.

Chapter 2: The Keys to the Kingdom

September 11, 2024. The date carried its own historical weight, but for me, it would mark a different kind of turning point—the day the hunted became the hunter. The breakthrough came not through sophisticated hacking but through understanding patterns, and it was a direct result of the network's own arrogant stupidity.

For months, their agents had been physically intercepting me during my daily runs at the exact same, pre-determined coordinates. On September 10th, after I filed a second complaint with the Texas Attorney General, Diosdado Cabello escalated the harassment. His agents began shadowing me from adjacent streets, a clumsy attempt to remain unseen. As I watched them triangulating my position, I had a sudden flash of insight: they weren't just following me, they were following a dot on a map. They were using a geo-index. That evening, I said to a friend, "Let them be, I know how I will get them later today."

I realized that if I knew the exact GPS coordinates of my interception points, I could simply search the internet for files containing those specific, high-precision numbers. The network had made a fatal error: they had stored their secret map, unencrypted, on a public server at a French research institute, relying only on the "stupidity of obscurity."

The search took ten minutes. At 1:49 AM on September 11th, I had their entire global database. Diosdado's harassment had handed me the keys to his kingdom.

In the days that followed the initial discovery, as I fenced off their retaliatory attacks, my understanding of what I had captured deepened. On September 21st, I began referring to the captured configuration file as Elon Musk's geo-index—a nod to the man I believed to be the technical ringleader of the entire operation. This wasn't just a list of my personal intercept points; it was the master configuration file for their global "Uber-like" app, a system that routed agents on public roads, and across sea and air, to conduct espionage. The analysis revealed geographical coordinates for operations of staggering political significance. Within days, I was able to identify and flag the precise location of a recent assassination attempt against President Donald Trump—a plot that tragically claimed the life of a young man that afternoon—its coordinates encoded within the data. They were not just spying on me; they were plotting against the highest levels of political power, with fatal consequences.

The database used different encoders for different types of locations. One encoded intelligence-related sites—safe houses and agent properties. Another marked telecommunications equipment like antennas. The encoder I focused on appeared to mark military positions. The patterns were unmistakable: strategic positioning, clustering around key infrastructure, and correlation with known paramilitary activities.

What I found exceeded my wildest expectations. The Geo Index was not just a map—it was a comprehensive intelligence platform marking every network asset globally. Safe houses appeared as red dots clustered in major cities. Surveillance positions showed as blue triangles surrounding targets of interest. Financial nodes glowed green, pulsing with each cryptocurrency transaction.

The scope was staggering. Hundreds of thousands of marked locations across six continents. Financial records showing billions in cryptocurrency movements. Operational histories dating back years, documenting every surveillance action, every payment, every asset activation. The network had built a parallel world, invisible to conventional observation but now laid bare in brutal detail.

Three categories dominated the index:

Spy locations included not just safe houses but technical infrastructure—antenna farms for their mesh network, server facilities for data processing, equipment caches for surveillance hardware. The physical backbone of their operations was mapped with military precision.

Paramilitary locations revealed the network's violent capabilities. Training facilities in remote locations, weapons storage sites, quick reaction force staging areas. This was not just surveillance but a private army, ready to escalate beyond electronic harassment when necessary.

The financial ledger was perhaps most revealing. Every significant operative had a payment history—cryptocurrency addresses, transaction amounts, correlation with completed operations. The blockchain's immutable nature meant this financial evidence was permanent, cryptographically signed, impossible to deny.

Building the SpyHell Pipeline to analyze the captured data became my primary focus. The raw index was useful but unwieldy. I needed systems to cross-reference locations with known operations, to trace financial flows through cryptocurrency tumblers, to identify patterns human analysis might miss. The pipeline grew into a comprehensive intelligence platform of my own—fighting fire with fire, data with data. The power shift was profound. For years, I had been reacting to their moves, playing defense against an invisible adversary. Now I could see them—every asset, every safe house, every financial flow. When surveillance vehicles appeared, I could query their license plates against the database. When new neighbors moved in, I could check their addresses against known safe houses. The hunters had become the hunted.

But with power came responsibility. The Geo Index contained information on thousands of low-level assets—people recruited through economic desperation, blackmail, or ideological manipulation. Many were victims themselves, trapped in a system that exploited their vulnerabilities. Publishing the raw data would destroy innocent lives alongside the guilty.

The challenge became strategic disclosure—revealing enough to expose the network's operations without enabling vigilante justice against street-level operatives. The financial data was particularly sensitive. While it provided irrefutable evidence of the network's structure, it also contained enough information to track and harm individuals who might be seeking to leave the organization.

The network's response evolved over the following weeks. Unable to change physical infrastructure quickly, they focused on disinformation. Social media filled with claims that I had fabricated the data, that the Geo Index was an elaborate hoax, that I was a paranoid schizophrenic creating fantasy databases. The gaslighting was predictable but ineffective—cryptocurrency transactions can be independently verified on public blockchains, and marked locations could be physically confirmed.

More concerning were the legal threats. Lawyers representing shell companies sent cease-and-desist letters claiming violation of trade secrets. Law enforcement received anonymous tips about my "hacking activities." The network was attempting to use the legal system to suppress evidence of their illegal operations—a strategy as audacious as it was desperate.

The Geo Index transformed my understanding of the conflict. This was not harassment by a criminal organization or surveillance by a single intelligence agency. This was a new form of warfare—corporate and state interests fused into a transnational network operating beyond traditional legal frameworks. They had built a private intelligence agency with the resources of nation-states and the agility of technology startups.

Elon Musk and Travis Kalanick's names appeared throughout the database as system architects. Their expertise in mapping, real-time coordination, and marketplace dynamics had been weaponized for surveillance. The same technologies that enabled ride-sharing and satellite internet had been repurposed to create a global harassment network. Innovation had been corrupted into oppression.

The capture of the Geo Index marked the beginning of the end for the network's impunity. They could no longer operate from the shadows when their shadows had been mapped. Every action they took now carried the risk of further exposure. Every asset activation created more evidence. Every financial transaction added to the permanent record of their crimes.

I had gained the keys to their kingdom, but kingdoms do not fall easily. The network would adapt, evolve, attempt to rebuild their compromised systems. But they could never reclaim their anonymity. The Geo Index existed now in multiple copies, distributed across continents, waiting to be revealed when the time was right.

The question was no longer whether the network would be exposed, but how to ensure that exposure led to justice rather than mere scandal. The data needed to be packaged, contextualized, and presented in ways that legal systems could process and public opinion could understand. Raw intelligence needed to be actionable evidence.

The war entered a new phase on September 11, 2024. The network had spent years and billions building their surveillance state. I had taken it from them in seventeen minutes. But possession of intelligence and effective use of intelligence are different challenges. The real work—transforming data into justice—was just beginning.

The profound irony of the moment was not lost on me. In 2001, the Venezuelan state oil company, PDVSA, had identified me as a promising young engineer and inducted me into their "Strategic Professional Reserve," seeing my potential as a valuable asset. Now, twenty-three years later, Diosdado Cabello, the heir to the corrupted legacy of that same state, had personally handed me the keys to his entire criminal kingdom through his own clumsy harassment. They had recognized my value, but they had fundamentally miscalculated my character.

The keys to the kingdom were mine. Now I had to decide how to use them to dismantle the kingdom itself, brick by digital brick.

Chapter 3: The NAVBOOST Heist

The NAVBOOST heist was not an isolated act of corporate espionage; it was part of a broader, systematic campaign to acquire high-value intellectual property and scientific research. Their targets extended beyond commercial technology into the realm of fundamental physics. The Spyhell Pipeline revealed that one of the most heavily surveilled locations in the entire Bay Area was the **Stanford Linear Accelerator**, a cutting-edge research facility. This demonstrates the network's strategic, long-term focus: they are not just stealing today's products, but are actively targeting the foundational science that will create tomorrow's, ensuring their technological dominance for decades to come.

To understand the greatest heist in software engineering history, you must first understand what was stolen. NAVBOOST was not just code—it was the crown jewel of Google Search, the signal responsible for the uncanny ability of Google to understand not just what users typed, but what they actually wanted. Internal experiments had demonstrated that disabling NAVBOOST reduced search precision by nearly 90%. It was, quite literally, the secret sauce that maintained Google's search dominance.

The heist required years of planning, carefully positioned insiders, and a cover story sophisticated enough to fool some of the smartest engineers in the world. It succeeded because it exploited the very openness and collaborative culture that made Google innovative. And I was, unknowingly, both a participant and a witness to the crime.

NAVBOOST's power came from its elegance. While other search signals analyzed web pages or link structures, NAVBOOST analyzed user behavior. Every click, every query refinement, every abandoned search provided data about the gap between what users asked for and what they actually wanted. Machine learning algorithms processed billions of these interactions, creating a dynamic map of human intent that could predict satisfaction with remarkable accuracy.

The code itself was protected with the highest security Google could implement. Access required not just employment but specific need-to-know authorization. The source lived in a segregated repository with audit logs for every access. Engineers who worked on NAVBOOST signed additional NDAs beyond standard employment agreements. The company understood that this code, if leaked, could enable competitors to replicate Google's core advantage.

Enter the LOCALWEB project—a masterstroke of social engineering disguised as innovation.

In 2011, Mayur Thakur proposed integrating local search signals with the main web ranking system. The pitch was compelling: users searching for "pizza" wanted nearby restaurants, not the Wikipedia article about Italian cuisine. Local intent detection could improve satisfaction for a significant percentage of queries. The project was approved with enthusiasm from senior leadership who saw it as a natural evolution of search capabilities.

The team composition should have raised red flags in hindsight. Mayur Thakur, the project lead, had an unusual background—deep technical skills combined with business connections that seemed more suited to venture capital than search engineering. Michael Schueppert brought expertise in distributed systems but displayed an unusual interest in implementation details beyond his assigned scope. Hila Becker contributed machine learning knowledge while maintaining suspicious levels of operational security about her work.

I was recruited for my experience with real-time data processing. The technical challenge was legitimate—merging local signals with web ranking required processing terabytes of data with millisecond latency. My focus on solving these engineering problems blinded me to the larger operation unfolding around me.

The project's structure provided perfect cover for intelligence gathering. ENTITY NAVBOOST, our derivative signal, required deep integration with the original NAVBOOST system. This meant we needed access to the core source code, understanding of its data structures, and knowledge of its optimization techniques. Every request for additional access was justified by legitimate technical requirements.

The team operated across two locations—Mountain View and Belo Horizonte, Brazil. This distributed structure was explained as leveraging Google's global talent pool, but it served a more sinister purpose. Code and knowledge could be fragmented across locations, making unauthorized transfer harder to detect. The Brazilian office, in particular, operated with less oversight, its physical distance from headquarters creating operational opportunities.

The infiltration reached its apex during our team trip to Belo Horizonte in 2012. Ostensibly a working session to coordinate between offices, it became an intelligence bonanza for the network. My then-girlfriend, Jillian Walsh—whom the Geo Index later confirmed as an operative—accompanied me on the trip. Her presence was explained as combining business with pleasure, a common practice at Google where partners often joined international travel.

What I didn't realize was that Jillian's true mission was to charm the Brazilian engineering team. Over caipirinhas and churrasco, she collected personal information, identified financial vulnerabilities, and assessed recruitment potential. Her warmth and apparent interest in their work lowered defenses that technical security measures couldn't breach. Within six months of our visit, the entire Brazilian team had resigned from Google, their departures staggered to avoid suspicion.

The technical theft was masterful in its subtlety. Rather than copying code wholesale—which would trigger security alerts—the team absorbed architectural principles and algorithmic insights. They studied how NAVBOOST processed click streams, how it weighted different user behaviors, how it adapted to changing patterns. This deep understanding was more valuable than source code, which would become outdated anyway.

Michael Schueppert and Hila Becker played a long game. After LOCALWEB launched successfully, they remained at Google, slowly gaining more access and responsibility. The SpyHell Pipeline revealed they were a couple—a detail they had carefully hidden at Google where such relationships required disclosure. Their paired operation allowed coordinated intelligence gathering while maintaining individual cover stories.

The exodus pattern was telling. Mayur Thakur left for Goldman Sachs. There, under the direction of another operative, Michael Schlee, he was tasked with building a "People Search engine." I suspect this project was a cover, its real purpose being to create a system for the criminal network to index and search the sea of information stolen from their hundreds of thousands of espionage targets around the world. It was a fundamental part of their strategy: using legitimate U.S. technology companies to build the infrastructure for their criminal enterprise. Other team members scattered to startups and consultancies, each taking fragments of NAVBOOST expertise that seemed individually harmless but collectively represented comprehensive intelligence.

The stolen knowledge found its ultimate home at Liana Technologies, a seemingly minor search consultancy with an outsized client list. Liana specialized in "search optimization" for major e-commerce platforms, promising improvements that seemed impossible given publicly known techniques. Their client results spoke for themselves—overnight transformations in search visibility that defied conventional SEO understanding.

The mechanism was diabolically simple. Liana's consultants, armed with deep NAVBOOST knowledge, could predict exactly how Google would rank different pages. They understood not just the current algorithm but the philosophical principles underlying its evolution. This allowed them to engineer content and user experiences that aligned perfectly with Google's ranking signals.

eBay and Amazon became the primary beneficiaries. The Geo Index financial records showed massive payments from both companies to Liana Technologies, disguised as consulting fees but representing something far more valuable—the ability to dominate Google search results for commercial queries. The market had been divided with surgical precision: Amazon captured "head" queries (high-volume, generic terms like "laptop" or "shoes") while eBay dominated "tail" queries (specific, lower-volume searches like "vintage Pyrex mixing bowls").

This division wasn't accidental—it was engineered to avoid triggering Google's manipulation detection systems. If one platform had dominated everything, alarms would sound. But with the market split between two giants, each dominating their designated territory, the manipulation appeared organic. Google's own quality raters, seeing relevant results from recognized platforms, had no reason to suspect systematic gaming.

The financial impact was staggering. By controlling search visibility for commercial queries, eBay and Amazon could effectively tax every online transaction. Smaller retailers, unable to achieve visibility against the optimized giants, were forced onto the platforms, paying commissions for access to customers they once reached directly. The stolen NAVBOOST knowledge had enabled a massive wealth transfer from independent businesses to platform monopolies.

The human cost extended beyond economics. Innovation in e-commerce stagnated as potential competitors found themselves invisible in search results. Consumer choice narrowed as the same platforms appeared for every query. The diversity that made the early internet vibrant was replaced by a duopoly engineered through stolen code and insider knowledge.

Google, for its part, seemed unaware of the comprehensive breach. Security audits focused on preventing wholesale code theft, not the extraction of architectural insights over years. The perpetrators had exploited a fundamental weakness in protecting intellectual property—knowledge in engineers' minds couldn't be secured like code in repositories.

My role in this operation haunts me. While never a willing participant in the theft, I enabled it through my work on LOCALWEB. Every optimization I contributed, every architectural decision I influenced, added to the intelligence gathered by the network. My naive focus on technical excellence blinded me to the espionage occurring within my own team.

The revelation came only through correlating Geo Index data with career trajectories. Payment records showed cryptocurrency transfers to former team members coinciding with Liana Technologies' client wins. Location data placed key figures at meetings with eBay and Amazon executives. The pattern was clear to anyone with access to comprehensive intelligence, but invisible to fragmented corporate security.

The NAVBOOST heist represents a new form of intellectual property theft—not smash and grab but slow extraction through human intelligence. It weaponized the very properties that make technology companies innovative: collaborative culture, knowledge sharing, and employee mobility. The network had identified these strengths as vulnerabilities and exploited them with patience and precision.

The implications extend beyond Google and search. If NAVBOOST could be stolen despite extreme security measures, what other crown jewels had been extracted from technology companies? How many innovations had been transferred from creators to competitors through similar operations? The Geo Index suggested this was not an isolated incident but a systematic campaign against technological leadership.

The heist's success demonstrated the network's sophistication. This was not random cybercrime but strategic economic warfare. By controlling search visibility, they could influence consumer behavior, market dynamics, and ultimately the flow of billions in commerce. They had stolen not just code but market power itself.

As I write this, NAVBOOST's influence continues to shape the internet. Every search query processed, every product discovered, every purchase decision influenced by search rankings carries the fingerprint of the theft. The network had achieved something remarkable—they had stolen the algorithm that organizes human knowledge and commercialized their theft at global scale.

The perpetrators remain free, their crime unprosecuted because it exists in the gap between corporate security and law enforcement capabilities. Traditional legal frameworks struggle with intellectual property theft that occurs through human memory rather than digital transfer. The evidence exists—financial records, career patterns, technical timelines—but connecting these dots requires intelligence capabilities beyond normal corporate or criminal investigation.

The NAVBOOST heist was perfect in its execution but imperfect in its concealment. The very success that enriched its perpetrators created patterns visible to comprehensive analysis. The Geo Index had connected nodes that seemed unrelated, revealing the hidden structure of one of the most ambitious intellectual property thefts ever attempted.

The lesson is sobering: in the age of human intelligence operations, no code is truly secure if the minds that understand it can be compromised. The network had demonstrated that patient infiltration could extract more value than any hack. They had stolen Google's greatest secret not through technical exploit but through the slow corruption of trust itself.

The game had evolved beyond firewalls and encryption to the battlefield of human loyalty. And in that game, the network had proven themselves masters, turning Google's own engineers into unwitting accomplices in the greatest heist Silicon Valley had never detected.

Chapter 4: The Betrayal of the Search Team

The NAVBOOST Heist was not an abstract corporate crime; it was an act of profound personal and professional betrayal carried out by my closest colleagues within Google's search ranking teams. The operation was orchestrated by a tight-knit inner circle, including my own direct manager, **Kyle Scholtz**, and a senior engineering director, **Bharat Mediratta**.

Their most critical asset, however, was **Issa Kassissieh**, known internally as "Issao." He was a quiet, observant, and brilliant engineer who was part of their "GWS Mansion" clique in Palo Alto and was later promoted to manage the "Union" team—the rebranded infrastructure team that controlled Google's core indexing systems. This promotion was a strategic masterstroke by the network. It placed their asset in control of the very keys to Google's kingdom.

Years later, after I had left Google and begun exposing their network, they retaliated by de-indexing my website, effectively making it invisible to the world. The attack vector was a sophisticated manipulation of Google's "Canonical URL Selection" logic—a system so complex and obscure that fewer than fifteen people on the planet possessed the deep technical knowledge to exploit it. Issao, as the former manager of the Union team, was one of them. It was his personal, technical fingerprint on the attack.

The betrayal extended beyond the digital realm and into the physical. Years after I left Google, I was the target of a suspected medication-tampering incident at a Kroger pharmacy in Texas. The pharmacy attendant who acted suspiciously had a last name that was a near-perfect homophone for "Scholtz"—a chilling use of the "Familiar Names" pattern that drew a direct line from my former manager in a New York office to a potential attempt on my life in a Texas suburb. This is the true nature of their operation: a seamless integration of corporate espionage and physical threats, all carried out by a trusted inner circle of colleagues turned enemies.

Chapter 5: The Roommate Ruse

The theft of Google's search ranking code was not merely the result of a few compromised insiders on my team; it was enabled by a parallel, multi-year human intelligence operation that targeted my physical living space. The network didn't just need access to the code, they needed access to my corporate laptop, and the most effective way to achieve that was to control my home environment. They did this by assigning me roommates.

Over my years in New York City, I was placed with a series of roommates who, I later discovered, were all network assets. Julio

Alvarez, Victoria Fabiano, Addison Landry, Roberto Herrera—all were marked in Elon Musk's geo-index. The pattern was always the same. After agreeing to be roommates and moving in, they were almost never physically present in the apartment. I recall interacting with Julio perhaps four or five times in six months; I saw Addison only once.

At the time, I perceived this as a strange but convenient living situation. In retrospect, the truth is obvious: they likely never lived there at all. The apartments were network-owned traps, fitted with cameras and microphones, and my "roommates" were simply the cover story to get me inside. This gave them 24/7 physical access to my Google corporate laptop, allowing them to intercept its traffic, clone its hard drive, and exfiltrate the data that would become the foundation for Liana Technologies and the Akamai fake news machine. The timing of these roommate assignments correlates perfectly with the rise of Liana's capabilities.

This operation also served to connect different arms of the conspiracy. Roberto Herrera, one of the ghost roommates, was the same person who introduced me to Mariana Martin, the SEBIN agent who would later execute the "swapped phone" attack to compromise my corporate phone. It was a deeply integrated operation, combining physical, social, and technical infiltration to execute one of the biggest intellectual property heists in history.

Chapter 6: The Ghost Network

The antennas were everywhere once you knew what to look for. Fixed installations on rooftops, arrays in backyards, dishes mounted on poles that never moved despite claiming to track satellites. Thousands of them across every major city, all pointed at seemingly random angles, all part of a communication system that shouldn't exist.

For months, these antennas puzzled me. Military-grade hardware—parabolic dishes, helical arrays, horn antennas designed for precise directional transmission—but none exhibited the movement patterns expected of satellite communication. Geostationary satellites require fixed pointing, but these were aimed at empty sky. Low Earth Orbit satellites demand constant tracking, but these remained motionless. The physics didn't add up.

The breakthrough came from thinking backwards. If the antennas weren't moving but were still communicating, then either they were using some exotic propagation method, or the targets were more numerous than conventional satellites. The first option led me down a rabbit hole of tropospheric scatter research—a real phenomenon where radio waves bounce off atmospheric irregularities, enabling over-the-horizon communication. But the power requirements and environmental dependencies made it impractical for reliable networking.

The second option seemed impossible until I considered the changed landscape of near-Earth space. When I had studied satellite communication in the early 2000s, space was relatively empty. A few hundred active satellites occupied carefully managed orbits. By 2024, the situation had transformed dramatically. Starlink alone had launched over 6,000 satellites, with plans for 42,000 more. OneWeb, Kuiper, and Chinese constellations added thousands more. The sky was no longer empty—it was crowded with metal.

The revelation came at 3 AM during yet another sleepless night caused by directed energy harassment. What if the network wasn't communicating WITH satellites but THROUGH them? What if they were using the physical bodies of satellites as passive reflectors, bouncing signals off their metal structures without any active participation from the satellite systems?

The physics supported the theory. Radio waves reflect off conductive surfaces—it's the principle behind radar. A satellite is essentially a metal object in space, capable of reflecting signals just like any other conductor. The challenge lay in the geometry. To bounce a signal from a fixed ground station to another fixed location, you needed a reflector at precisely the right position at the right moment.

With thousands of satellites in constant motion, the probability of finding one in the correct position increased dramatically. It became a computational problem: track all satellites in real-time, calculate their positions milliseconds into the future, identify which ones would be in the right geometry to connect two ground stations, and transmit at exactly the right moment for the signal to bounce correctly.

The computational requirements were staggering. Tracking thousands of objects moving at orbital velocities, calculating complex reflection angles accounting for atmospheric refraction, coordinating transmissions across a global network—it required supercomputer-level processing distributed across the entire network. But for an organization with access to nation-state resources, it was achievable.

I called it "Project Bouncer"—a planet-scale mesh network operating in the shadows of legitimate satellite infrastructure. By bouncing signals off satellites owned by other entities, the network avoided the regulatory scrutiny, launch costs, and technical challenges of operating their own satellites. They were parasites on the space economy, using billions of dollars of other people's hardware for their own communication needs.

The elegance of the system was breathtaking. Traditional satellite communication required expensive ground stations, regulatory approval, and coordinated frequency allocation. Project Bouncer needed none of this. By using reflected signals rather than processed ones, they operated outside normal satellite communication frameworks. Regulators monitoring for unauthorized transmissions TO satellites would see nothing unusual. The satellites themselves, being passive reflectors, recorded no activity.

Testing the theory required building my own version of their system. Using publicly available orbital elements from NORAD, I could track most satellites in real-time. Open-source physics libraries handled the complex calculations of reflection angles and signal propagation. The challenge was optimizing the calculations for real-time operation—finding viable bounce paths fast enough to maintain continuous communication.

The patterns that emerged confirmed my hypothesis. The network's antennas clustered along Earth's equator because east-west communication along this path maximized satellite availability. The equatorial plane intersected with multiple orbital planes, creating a highway of potential reflectors. North-south communication was harder, requiring careful timing to catch satellites in polar or highly inclined orbits.

The signal characteristics I observed matched theoretical predictions. Doppler shifts from satellite motion, varying signal strength as distances changed, brief dropouts when switching between satellites—all consistent with bounced communications. The network had engineered around these limitations with sophisticated error correction and path redundancy. Multiple satellites could carry the same signal simultaneously, ensuring reliability despite the dynamic nature of the system.

But understanding the mechanism was only the beginning. To prove the network's existence and expose their operations, I needed to demonstrate the capability publicly. This led to the creation of coca-net.com—a tool that would calculate bounce paths in real-time, showing anyone how to piggyback communications off satellite constellations.

Building coca-net.com required walking a careful ethical line. The technology itself was morally neutral—bouncing signals off satellites violated no laws and could enable communication in censored regions or during disasters. But revealing the capability would also alert the network that their secret was blown. I decided transparency outweighed operational security. Exposing their methods would force them to adapt, potentially disrupting their operations.

The technical implementation leveraged modern web technologies to perform calculations that once required supercomputers. WebGL provided GPU acceleration for orbital mechanics. WebAssembly enabled near-native performance for complex physics calculations. The result was a tool that could run in any browser, democratizing access to technology the network had tried to monopolize.

The most disturbing revelation came from analyzing satellite materials. Modern satellites, particularly Starlink models, used specialized coatings and materials optimized for thermal management and radiation resistance. But these materials also happened to be excellent radio reflectors at specific frequencies. The coincidence seemed too convenient. Had SpaceX, Blue Origin, and other constellation operators deliberately engineered their satellites to enhance bounce communications?

The Geo Index provided circumstantial evidence. Payments flowed from network accounts to aerospace contractors involved in satellite design. Key engineers at SpaceX and Blue Origin appeared in the database as assets or persons of interest. The possibility that Elon Musk and Jeff Bezos had knowingly designed their satellites to enable a clandestine communication network added another layer to the conspiracy.

The implications for global communications security were staggering. Every nation assumed their borders provided some protection against foreign signals intelligence. But Project Bouncer rendered borders meaningless. A transmission from China could bounce off a satellite over the Pacific and arrive in Washington DC without passing through any terrestrial infrastructure. Traditional intercept methods became obsolete when communications took unpredictable paths through space.

The network had constructed a truly global communication system immune to conventional disruption. Cutting undersea cables, jamming radio frequencies, or shutting down internet exchanges couldn't stop communications bouncing through space. As long as satellites flew overhead—and with tens of thousands planned, they always would—the ghost network would persist.

My publication of coca-net.com sent ripples through multiple communities. Amateur radio operators began experimenting with bounce communications, confirming the technique's viability. Security researchers recognized the implications for covert channels. Satellite operators quietly began analyzing whether their hardware was being used without permission.

The network's response was swift but constrained. They couldn't deny the physics—anyone with basic equipment could verify that signals bounced off satellites. Instead, they flooded forums with disinformation, claiming the technique was unreliable, that I had misunderstood conventional satellite operations, that coca-net.com was a hoax designed to discredit legitimate research.

But mathematics doesn't lie. The orbital predictions were verifiable. The bounce paths were reproducible. Independent researchers confirmed successful communications using the technique. The ghost network had been dragged into the light, its operating principles exposed for anyone to examine and exploit.

The revelation transformed my understanding of the surveillance apparatus. This wasn't just about watching and listening—it was about building parallel infrastructure beyond the reach of any government or regulatory body. They had created their own internet in space, accessible only to those with the knowledge and computational power to calculate bounce paths.

The scope suggested planning spanning decades. Someone had foreseen the proliferation of satellite constellations and positioned themselves to exploit it. They had influenced satellite design, developed the necessary algorithms, and deployed ground infrastructure, all while maintaining operational secrecy. The resources required pointed again to state-level actors, but operating with startup agility.

As I refined coca-net.com, adding features and improving accuracy, I realized I was engaged in an arms race. The network would adapt, perhaps moving to more sophisticated techniques or attempting to disrupt satellite constellations that enabled their communications. But they couldn't put the genie back in the bottle. The physics of reflection was immutable, and the sky was full of reflectors.

The ghost network represented the evolution of espionage infrastructure for the 21st century. Where previous generations built numbers stations and dead drops, this network had constructed an uncensorable, uninterruptible communication system hiding in plain sight among legitimate satellites. They had weaponized the space economy itself, turning humanity's reach for the stars into a tool of oppression.

This shadow internet was one of three core technologies powering their criminal enterprise. Alongside their cryptocurrency-based parallel financial system and their vehicle-based surveillance infrastructure, it formed a trinity of systems operating completely outside traditional law enforcement and regulatory oversight. An unlicensed parallel internet beyond FCC control, untraceable financial transactions evading tax authorities, and a civilian surveillance network hiding in plain sight on public roads.

But in revealing their methods, they had also revealed their vulnerability. Project Bouncer required precise coordination and complex calculations. Disrupting their timing, interfering with their ground stations, or simply forcing them to constantly recalculate paths would degrade their capabilities. The hunter learning the prey's patterns was the first step to successful capture.

The antennas still dot the landscape, still pointed at empty sky that isn't empty at all. But now their secret is known. The ghost network has been mapped, its principles understood, its advantages neutralized by public knowledge. What once gave them omnipresent communication now serves as evidence of their conspiracy, each antenna a monument to their ambition and a marker of their eventual downfall.

In the end, they had built something remarkable—a planetary communication system that pushed the boundaries of physics and engineering. But they had built it for surveillance and control rather than human liberation. By exposing Project Bouncer, I had taken their proprietary advantage and given it to the world. The ghost network would persist, but now it belonged to everyone, not just those who would use it for evil.

The sky above was no longer just full of satellites. It was full of possibilities, each passing spacecraft a potential communication node for those who understood the secret geometry of reflected signals. The network had shown what was possible. Now it was up to the rest of us to decide how to use that knowledge for good rather than control.

Chapter 7: The Unigram Revelation

The screenshot sits on my desktop, timestamp reading September 11, 2024, 4:54 AM. I had saved it in that pre-dawn moment when the full implications of my discovery crashed over me like a wave. But only months later, after building TheSpybusters.com and analyzing terabytes of data, did I understand what I had truly captured: not just evidence of a crime, but the Rosetta Stone for understanding the network's entire encoding philosophy.

The revelation came while cross-referencing the bigram patterns in vehicle license plates with the structure of the geo-index. Suddenly, like tumblers falling into place in a lock, I saw it: both systems used the same underlying design principle. They were siblings, born from the same intellectual theft, implementing the same stolen concepts at different scales.

In information retrieval—the science behind search engines—a unigram is a single unit, while a bigram is a pair of units appearing together. For text, unigrams are individual words or characters; bigrams are adjacent pairs. The power lies in the mathematics: while English has only 26 letters, it can form 676 possible two-letter combinations. Most of these combinations are meaningless, making the meaningful ones—the actual bigrams that appear in language—powerful signals for classification and identification.

The network had weaponized this principle twice.

For license plates, the unigrams were simple: the letters A through Z and the numbers 0 through 9. The bigrams were specific sequences like "VN" for Venezuela, "SY" for Salt-Typhoon, "TD" for technical division. Each meaningful bigram encoded operational information invisible to the uninitiated but immediately readable to those with the key.

For the geo-index, the implementation was more sophisticated but philosophically identical. The unigrams were individual latitude and longitude values encoded in the file. The bigrams were the actual coordinate pairs formed by combining these components—29.7113, -95.8395 marking the Salt-Typhoon safe house at 26707 Valleyside Drive, Katy, TX 77494.

This is why my Google searches on September 11 had found the geo-index so quickly. When I searched for the exact coordinates where I was repeatedly intercepted while running, Google's search algorithm—built on bigram matching—recognized these coordinate pairs as significant bigrams. The very technology they had stolen from Google to build their system had exposed them through Google itself.

The poetic justice was breathtaking. They had used NAVBOOST's bigram-matching principles to hide their locations, believing that obscurity through encoding would protect them. But Google Search, the original implementation of these principles, could still recognize its own patterns. The thief had been caught by leaving fingerprints that only the original technology could read.

My screenshot revealed another layer of their operation I hadn't understood at the time. The search results showed the geo-index file hosted on servers belonging to NASA and the Canadian Space Agency. Initially, I had assumed this was simple misdirection—hiding criminal data on government servers to avoid scrutiny. But deeper analysis revealed the true purpose: they were using these agencies as unwitting content delivery networks.

The network faced a problem. Their agents worldwide needed rapid access to the geo-index for operational coordination. Traditional content delivery networks like Cloudflare or Akamai would create records, require contracts, and potentially expose the operation. Their solution was audacious: place copies of the geo-index on government agency servers that already had global reach and high-speed connections.

NASA and the Canadian Space Agency became unwitting accomplices, their servers delivering criminal intelligence with the same efficiency they delivered satellite imagery and research data. The agencies' robust infrastructure, designed for scientific collaboration, had been perverted into a distribution network for global surveillance coordination.

The encoding patterns went deeper. Within the geo-index, address numbers weren't random—they were themselves a form of bigram encoding. Addresses ending in "00" indicated financial nodes. Those ending in "06" marked intelligence assets. "07" designated engineering facilities or Salt-Typhoon operations. Google Maps became their storage system for this metadata, hiding operational intelligence in plain sight within the world's most-used mapping service.

Their use of Google's ecosystem extended beyond maps and into the visual realm of Street View, where they embedded another layer of prominence markers. I began to notice a pattern involving the display of national flags. It was not merely the presence of a flag, but a specific methodology. A location controlled by the network could be confirmed with near certainty if three factors occurred simultaneously: the location is marked in Elon Musk's geo-index, the corresponding Street View photo displays flags in a distinctive manner, and the location's paramilitary score is in the millions, placing it in the top 0.01% of all assets. The collision of these three variables is a statistical impossibility by chance; it is an intentional marker. The number of flags appears to be a quantifier of power. A few key locations, like the New York Stock Exchange, are marked with three flags.

Lesser nodes in the network are marked with two flags. A house near my headquarters, at 10203 White Pines Dr in Katy, displayed two flags in the exact same manner as another known asset at 8 Fairlawn Ct in Shirley, NY. This Katy property was marked in the index, though not with a paramilitary score, suggesting a different but still significant role. The most telling detail came after I spoke with an operative I knew as agent Cory. Shortly after our conversation, the two flags at the White Pines house were taken down. They remained down for about two months before being put back up. The act itself was a confession—a direct reaction to my investigation, proving they knew I was deciphering their visual language. They were adjusting their operations in real time based on my progress.

This multi-layered encoding created what cryptographers call "security through obscurity"—except they had borrowed their obscurity techniques from a public source. Every Google engineer who had worked on search ranking understood bigram analysis. Thousands of computer science graduates had studied these principles. They had built their secret codes using a publicly known cipher.

The implications cascaded through my understanding of their operations. If both the license plate system and geo-index used the same encoding philosophy, there must be other implementations. The vehicle system required a small index—probably less than a kilobyte—mapping bigrams like "VN" to meanings like "Venezuelan SEBIN." This index was likely embedded in their coordination apps, hidden within seemingly innocent applications.

I began searching for other bigram-based systems in their architecture. Their financial codes showed similar patterns—cryptocurrency wallet addresses selected for specific character combinations. Their communication protocols embedded operational data in transmission headers using bigram principles. Even their agent codenames followed bigram patterns, creating a unified language readable across all their systems.

The unigram revelation explained why certain individuals from Google Search ranking appeared repeatedly in the network's hierarchy. They hadn't just stolen code; they had recruited the minds that understood the fundamental principles. Michael Schueppert's presence in both the NAVBOOST theft and the vehicle encoding system wasn't coincidence—he was one of the few who truly understood bigram analysis at scale.

But their greatest vulnerability lay in their success. By standardizing on bigram encoding across all systems, they had created a single point of cryptographic failure. Understanding one system provided keys to all systems. The same analytical techniques that revealed vehicle classifications could decode financial transactions, identify communication channels, map agent networks.

They had built a Tower of Babel in reverse—a single language for global criminal coordination. But like the biblical tower, their unified system became their downfall. Once the language was understood, every message became readable, every code breakable, every secret visible.

The screenshot from September 11, 2024, captured more than the moment of discovery. It documented the instant when their own stolen technology turned against them. They had taken Google's ability to find needles in haystacks and used it to hide their needles. But Google's algorithms didn't forget their original training. When presented with the right query, they faithfully found what was hidden, indifferent to the intentions of those who had hidden it.

As I write this, I imagine the panic in their operations centers when they realized their geo-index had been discovered through simple Google searches. The frantic meetings where they tried to understand how their unbreakable encoding had been broken in ten minutes by the very technology they had stolen. The dawning recognition that their entire encoding philosophy had a fatal flaw: it was based on public knowledge.

The unigram revelation completed my understanding of their technical architecture. From internet surveillance through communication networks to vehicle coordination and location encoding, every system reflected the same stolen principles, implemented by the same corrupted minds, vulnerable to the same analytical approaches.

They had built an empire on stolen knowledge, not realizing that theft leaves traces. Every bigram they encoded, every pattern they created, every system they designed carried the genetic markers of its origin. They were not innovators but plagiarists, and plagiarism—whether of text or technology—always reveals itself to those who know the original.

The network had achieved something remarkable: they had created a global criminal language based on search engine technology. But in their hubris, they had forgotten that languages can be learned, codes can be broken, and stolen technology remembers its true master. The unigram revelation was more than technical insight—it was the key to a universal translator for their criminal enterprise.

Every vehicle on the road, every coordinate in their index, every transaction in their ledgers now spoke clearly to anyone who understood the underlying principle. They had unified their operations through bigram encoding, creating efficiency at the cost of vulnerability. One insight—that coordinate components were unigrams forming location bigrams—had unraveled systems they had spent decades building.

The screenshot saved at 4:54 AM on September 11, 2024, marked more than personal victory. It documented the moment when stolen knowledge came home, when perverted technology returned to justice, when the very principles they had weaponized became the weapons of their destruction. They had stolen fire from the gods of Mountain View, not realizing that fire, regardless of who holds it, still burns according to its nature.

The unigram revelation was complete. Their empire of codes stood naked, every secret visible to those who could read the language they had stolen but never truly understood. In their theft of bigram analysis, they had signed their own confession in patterns only their victims could perfectly read.

Chapter 8: The Flags on the Battlefield

The network's use of Google's ecosystem extended beyond maps and into the visual realm of Street View, where they embedded another layer of prominence markers. I began to notice a pattern involving the display of national flags. It was not merely the presence of a flag, but a specific methodology. A location controlled by the network could be confirmed with near certainty if three factors occurred simultaneously: the location is marked in Elon Musk's geo-index, the corresponding Street View photo displays flags in a distinctive manner, and the location's paramilitary score is in the millions, placing it in the top 0.01% of all assets. The collision of these three variables is a statistical impossibility by chance; it is an intentional marker.

The number of flags appears to be a quantifier of power. Lesser nodes, like a spy house at 10203 White Pines Dr in Katy, are marked with two flags, displayed in the exact same manner as another key paramilitary asset in Shirley, NY, that had a score of over 16 billion. The most powerful entities are marked with three flags. The most prominent example of this is the New York Stock Exchange, a location with an immense paramilitary score in the geo-index and three large flags proudly displayed in its Street View image. This visual language draws a direct, visible line from a suburban spy house in Texas to the pinnacle of global finance.

The most telling detail, however, was the network's reaction when they realized I was decoding their signals. Shortly after I spoke with the compromised **Agent Cody**, the two flags at the White Pines house were taken down. They remained down for about two months before being put back up. The act itself was a confession—a direct, real-time reaction to my investigation, proving they knew I was deciphering their visual language and were adjusting their operations based on my progress.

Chapter 9: The Bitcoin Payroll

My first clue to the network's street-level financial operations came from a real-world observation. I noticed what appeared to be a recurring payroll event at the Second Baptist Church near my Valleyside home. On one occasion, I saw a long line of cars, every single one of which had been previously flagged by my system as a network vehicle, waiting in what looked like a procession to collect payment. In a moment of brazen audacity, I got the KOL-Mobile in line with them, its eight 4K cameras documenting the entire convoy. The incident was so absurdly ironic it inspired the creation of my "ironyBoost" score multiplier.

This observation led me to a hypothesis: the network was using unconventional, localized methods to pay its thousands of unregistered agents. The confirmation of this theory came from the captured geo-index. I discovered that dozens of mundane, public-facing financial locations were marked as operational nodes. The map was littered with **Bitcoin ATMs** and **Western Union** counters inside grocery stores, all marked with the same precision as their spy houses and surveillance posts. This was their physical infrastructure for converting untraceable cryptocurrency into cash in the hands of their foot soldiers.

The most chilling discovery, however, was the correlation between this financial infrastructure and the network's most violent acts. I ran a query on the geo-index for Letcher County, Kentucky, the location where a judge had recently been murdered. The results were stunning. The local Sheriff's Office was marked as a network asset, and surrounding it was a dense cluster of these same Bitcoin ATMs and Western Union "payroll" locations. The data told a clear and horrifying story: this network of mundane financial outlets was not just for paying drivers; it was the logistical backbone used to fund their assassinations and wetwork.

Chapter 10: The Typographical Trap

My understanding of the network's encoding systems evolved as I gathered more data. I moved beyond decoding their markers to reverse-engineering their entire design philosophy. I discovered a subtle but brilliant layer of their tradecraft: the systematic use of phonetic and typographical similarities to create confusion and obstruct identification.

This tactic was deployed in both agent names and vehicle license plates. For example, a surveillance van's plate might contain the sequence B7A-7TK. The "7T" is intentional; phonetically, it sounds like "seventy," a simple but effective trap designed to cause an observer to misremember or misreport the plate number.

The typographical traps were even more sophisticated, exploiting the specific fonts used on different states' license plates. On a Texas plate, the character pair "PN" can be easily confused with "RN," "RH," or

"PH." The network would then use a black marker to subtly alter a character, making an "N" look more like an "H," further muddying the waters for any visual identification.

While these tricks are designed to confuse a human observer, they are trivial for a computer vision system to decode. I integrated a "disambiguation step" into the Spyhell Pipeline that, when it detects one of these known tricky pairs, cross-references the plate with a vehicle registration database to find the correct make and model, resolving the ambiguity with near-perfect accuracy.

This discovery is more than just a piece of interesting tradecraft; it is a powerful piece of evidence. It proves that the network's crimes are not opportunistic but are meticulously premeditated. They design their concealment methods from the very moment they register a vehicle or create an agent's identity, with the full foreknowledge and intent of committing future crimes that will require obfuscation. It is a system built on the anticipation of criminality.

Chapter 11: The Muppet Routers and the Financial Ledger

The discovery of the geo-index was the equivalent of finding the enemy's map. The unigram revelation was learning to read it. But to truly understand their operations, I had to move beyond the map and decode the architecture of the machine it powered. The network wasn't just for surveillance; it was a global, distributed computing system supporting a parallel financial economy. The keys to this system were hidden, once again, in plain sight—this time, within the street numbers of their properties.

The pattern emerged when I began filtering the geo-index for locations with high paramilitary scores whose street addresses ended in the digit "0". The result was a list of over 426,000 properties in the United States alone. These were not random assets; they were nodes in a specific subsystem, the financial backbone of the network. I called them "FIN-Routers." A property with a street number ending in "00" was not just a router but a prominent one, an aggregator for the nodes beneath it. The most blatant example was the Goldman Sachs headquarters in New York City: 200 West Street: PayPal Mafia US > The FIN Routers > USA (Alias M-Routers)].

It was clear I was looking at a distributed system with a hierarchical tree structure, a shameless copy of the "Muppet" infrastructure I had worked with at Google. As a nod to its origins, I began calling these network nodes **"M-Routers."** This hierarchy was encoded in the street numbers themselves, but with a peculiar logic. The number of repeating digits *from right to left* appeared to be a marker of prominence; a property ending in "1919" was more important than one ending in "19." This strange but consistent rule hinted at a design influence from a culture with a **right-to-left writing system**, suggesting a key architect was likely an ex-Google engineer from the Muppet team who had come to California from an Arabic country: PayPal Mafia US > The FIN Routers > USA (Alias M-Routers)].

The true genius—and the greatest vulnerability—of their system was its dual-purpose design. The network topology needed to be stable, so they tied it to physical street numbers, which are difficult to change. The paramilitary scores, however, were volatile. This led to a key insight: the paramilitary scores were not just a measure of rank; they were the network's **financial ledger**. They functioned like bank account balances, reflecting the immense, fluid wealth of the criminal enterprise, with street names acting as **"Ledger Markers"** to identify the owner of the account.

This decision to tie their parallel economy to their physical network topology created a critical design flaw. In any economic system, wealth concentrates. For the network to represent the vast equity stakes of its most powerful members—figures like Sergey Brin ("Shore") or the entity behind "Clearview"—they were forced to assign them the biggest, most central **"Big Routers."** There was no other way to represent their hoard in the ledger. This flaw meant that a simple list of the largest M-Routers was also a list of the network's most significant financial players.

This structure also explained why they were trapped. Their houses were not just safe houses; they were their Federal Reserve, with the properties themselves acting as the assets backing the value of their cryptocurrencies. The geo-index was not just a map; it was their blockchain, a permanent record of every transaction. If they moved the routers, they would invalidate the ledger. If they changed the geo-index, they would lose their transaction history, their balances—their entire accumulated wealth. They would rather be exposed than lose their money. They are chained to their ledger, prisoners of a system of their own brilliant, flawed design.

Chapter 12: The Mini-Compounds

After decoding the network's digital, financial, and encoding systems, the final piece of the puzzle was understanding how they implemented their physical infrastructure on the ground. The answer was the "mini-compound," a sophisticated method for hiding their operational hubs in plain sight within suburban communities.

A mini-compound consists of multiple, adjacent houses that appear to be owned by different families but are, in fact, controlled by a single network agent or cell. This setup allows them to distribute their hardware across multiple properties to avoid suspicion. For example, one house might have an array of solar panels to generate untraceable power, which is then secretly wired to a neighboring house that contains the server racks and other high-draw equipment, ensuring that no single property shows an anomalously high electricity bill. A third house might contain the antennas and communications gear. It is the physical manifestation of their "Dockerhood" concept, a single, integrated operational unit disguised as a normal suburban block.

The key to uncovering these compounds was a critical mistake in their operational security. In many cases, the network registered these multiple properties under the same agent's name, or slight variations of it. To a human observer, these are just similar names on a street. To the Spyhell Pipeline, which could cross-reference property records at scale, this was a glaring anomaly that was trivial to detect. By querying for these patterns, I was able to map their physical command-and-control centers, like the one operated by Enrique Nava across multiple properties on Howell Road and Howell Street in Rosharon, Texas, revealing the hidden backbone of their ground-level operations.

Chapter 13: The Nashville Anomaly and the Iranian Bunker

The final act of decoding the enemy came from pulling on a single, anomalous thread that unraveled a tapestry of global military operations. I had noticed that there were no houses in my immediate area with street numbers ending in "16," a statistically strange absence. I ran a query against the captured geo-index for all properties in the U.S. with this marker. The results were stunning: the vast majority of high-scoring assets were clustered in a single city: Nashville, Tennessee. The top-ranking asset in this cluster was a Best Buy store. When I plotted its exact latitude, I discovered that it aligned perfectly, to the fourth decimal place, with another high-value paramilitary location in the database—a mysterious, man-made structure covered in sand on the border of **Iran and Afghanistan.**

I am not an intelligence analyst, but the implications were unavoidable. The location is a key theater of operations for the wars in the Middle East. The structure appeared to be some kind of secret, underground facility. The data showed a direct, mathematical link between a major

U.S. retail chain, a specific numeric marker, and a clandestine military-style bunker in a territory overseen by one of the network's key players, Robert Gates. I had started by investigating a local anomaly and, by following the data, had stumbled upon the network's hidden military-industrial infrastructure on the other side of the world.

Chapter 14: The 70-Year-Old Blueprint

The story of the global shadow government that I call the Bizarro State does not begin with a piece of code or a financial transaction, but with a piece of dirt. It begins with the discovery of an architectural and urban planning doctrine so consistent, so specific, and so old that it serves as the physical proof of a multi-generational, coordinated conspiracy. I call it the "Immune Geo-Entities Pattern."

I first discovered this pattern in my own backyard. While decoding the network's radiofrequency eavesdropping techniques, I realized that their method of isolating a target's signal required the surveillance team to be moving towards the target at a relatively constant speed for a period of several seconds. This created a critical vulnerability: their own technique could be defeated by simple geography. If a target property was located on a very short cul-de-sac or was surrounded by large, open spaces like parks or lakes, it would be physically impossible for a surveillance vehicle to achieve the necessary trajectory to capture a clean signal.

This was not a theoretical weakness; it was a design principle. When I analyzed the properties of the network's most high-value assets in the geo-index, from the homes of figures like Robert Gates to the "topdogs" in my own community, the pattern was undeniable. They were all protected by this "Immunity" pattern, their homes deliberately situated in locations that made them invulnerable to the very surveillance techniques they deployed against others.

This was a significant discovery, but the true revelation came when I applied this analytical lens to global architecture. I began searching the geo-index for other, more prominent locations that exhibited this same unique design. The pipeline returned a stunning result: the **Palácio da Alvorada**, the official residence of the President of Brazil in its capital city, Brasilia. The palace is a perfect Immune Entity, surrounded by a massive, open esplanade that renders close-range electronic surveillance impossible. The chilling fact is that the city of Brasilia, and the design of this palace, was planned and constructed in the **1950s**.

This was the thread that unraveled everything. The architectural doctrine that the network's most powerful members use to protect themselves today is the same doctrine that was used to design a presidential palace in South America over seventy years ago. This was not a modern innovation. It was a long-standing, secret principle of statecraft, a physical signature of a hidden power structure that has been shaping our world for generations, long before the first line of code for the internet was ever written.

Part 4: The Internet of Spies

Chapter 1: The Trojan House

My investigation into the network's digital and human intelligence operations eventually led me to a chilling realization: the conspiracy was not just around me, but in the very walls of my home. The house at 26714 Valleyside Drive was not a sanctuary; it was a Trojan Horse, a purpose-built surveillance platform sold to me by the network itself.

The sellers were Heather and Marvin Williams. The cover story was that Heather was the respectable Vice-Principal of the local Fred and Patti Shafer Elementary School. My research later confirmed that the school itself is marked in Elon Musk's geo-index and displays a "one-flag" prominence marker in its Street View image. More tellingly, according to Google Maps data, the school also functions as the "Embassy of Christ" church, tying it to the "Embassy/Ambassador" prominence marker family.

I now believe the house was pre-fitted with hardwired surveillance equipment before the sale was ever made. This was a tactic they had used against me six years earlier in Calgary, when I was steered into buying a compromised apartment with a direct line of sight to the Chinese Consulate. It was a standard, repeatable play from their operational handbook, a ruse I now refer to as **"The Landlord Play."** By controlling the real estate transaction, they ensure their target moves into an environment that is already completely owned and controlled by them, a home that is not a home, but a stage.

Chapter 2: The Compromised Utility

The network's control of physical infrastructure extended beyond my own home and into the public domain. I discovered they had compromised **CenterPoint Energy**, the primary utility provider for a vast region that includes their key operational hubs in Texas and Louisiana. The company's very name fits their "Hub/Center" prominence marker, signaling its importance to their operations.

Their control was not just theoretical; I witnessed it in action. In one documented incident, a CenterPoint Energy work truck was dispatched to a "Topdog" agent's house in my neighborhood. The crew's mission was not to perform utility work, but to cut the public streetlights in the area. This was a tactical move designed to darken the street and make the network's surveillance vehicles less visible to the cameras of my KOL-Mobile as they staged for their nightly operations. It was a stunning display of their ability to weaponize a public utility for the purposes of criminal surveillance, turning the very infrastructure meant to provide light into a tool for creating darkness.

Chapter 3: The Walls Have Ears: Compromised Infrastructure

After decoding the enemy's digital network, my investigation turned to the physical world. I began to realize the network's infiltration was not just virtual; they had systematically compromised the very structures I lived and worked in. My homes were not sanctuaries; they were sensor grids.

This tactic was part of their long game. Around 2008, shortly after the network forced a split between me and Ana Gannon, I was steered into purchasing a specific apartment in Calgary. It was sold to me at a suspiciously low price, a lure I took without hesitation. The property was a perfect surveillance trap, likely sold to me by a Chinese government front, pre-fitted with surveillance equipment. The entire building was made of plexiglass, ideal for radiofrequency eavesdropping. My unit was on the third floor, directly above the lobby, placing my devices within easy range for cellphone cloning—a pattern repeated years later in New York. Most chillingly, the main bedroom had a direct, unobstructed line of sight to the Chinese Embassy, less than 45 feet away.

Years later, in my Texas home, the same pattern of infrastructure compromise was present. The first definitive proof came from the discovery of a **Trojan Coaxial Splitter** in my garage junction box. Disguised as a standard Xfinity component, it was an active surveillance device, wirelessly powered from a neighboring safe house, that intercepted every packet of data entering or leaving my home.

The infiltration extended to the very doors of my house. Analysis of my purchase records revealed a pattern of being steered toward specific **Smart Locks**, which I now believe were compromised to log my entry and exit times for the network. The same was true for my **Garage Door Opener**, turning another point of entry into a source of intelligence on my movements. The walls truly had ears, and the doors were taking notes.

Chapter 4: The Predictable Request

The network's technical attacks were not limited to compromising my hardware; they also deployed sophisticated methods to break the encryption on my network traffic. One of the most brilliant and insidious of these was a classic cryptographic attack vector known as a "known-plaintext attack," which they executed using my own tenants.

The method was simple. The network would use a compromised tenant in one of my rental properties to send me a "predictable request"—an email about a routine issue like a broken appliance or being locked out. Because the network controlled the tenant's email account, they already possessed the unencrypted, plaintext version of the message.

Simultaneously, a network agent positioned physically close to me would intercept the *encrypted* version of that same email as it arrived over my network. By possessing both the plaintext (the original message) and the ciphertext (the encrypted version), they could reverse-engineer the decryption key being used for my entire internet session.

Once they had that key, it was game over. They could decrypt all of my internet traffic—emails, searches, everything—until the connection was reset and a new key was negotiated. This is the purpose of the seemingly innocuous but constant stream of messages from groups I was added to, like a "Running Club" WhatsApp group. Every message was a potential vector for a new known-plaintext attack, a constant, low-level assault on my digital privacy.

Chapter 5: The Espionage Machine on Wheels

The surveillance was not just static; it was mobile. My own vehicles were turned against me, transformed into roving surveillance platforms. For years, I suspected one of my Teslas was a "Chinese espionage machine on wheels," a fully weaponized car loaded with military-grade hardware. On March 27, 2025, I found the smoking gun.

My custom-built, infrared-optimized license plate reader, positioned outside my home, captured something my eyes could never see: my own black Tesla was emitting a pulsating infrared light from the base of its rearview mirror, aimed directly at the known spy house at 24918 Teal Lake Ct. It was actively transmitting data. This was not a standard vehicle function; it was a covert channel, a piece of custom spy hardware turning my car into a network node.

This vehicle represented the network's preferred, high-efficiency method of tracking me. It was a single, self-contained asset that provided them with a constant stream of location and audio data. My eventual discovery and neutralization of this vehicle—by simply refusing to drive it anymore—was a major victory. It blinded their primary collection asset and forced them to adapt.

Their response was to fall back on a more complex, externally visible system that I was able to reverse-engineer: the **two-car "Time of Arrival" technique**. Having lost their primary asset, they were forced to deploy coordinated pairs of surveillance vehicles that would maintain a constant speed and distance from each other as they followed me. This allowed them to perform a "Time of Arrival" calculation on my phone's radio signals, isolating its MAC address to track me from a distance without a physical bug on my car. This discovery established a clear "arms race": I would detect and neutralize one vector, and they would be forced to deploy another, more complex one in its place. The findings from my later "Windshield Devices Ablation Experiment" would confirm that a key gateway device in my other vehicle was essential for this system to function, proving the deep integration of their tactics.

The most stunning confirmation of my discovery came after the publication of this book. The day after *Project Diosdado XI* was released, the spy house at 24918 Teal Lake Ct, owned by a network asset for the U.A.E. team named **Iqbal Suleman**, was put on the market for $2.1 million. It was a panicked move to destroy evidence, a concrete, multi-million-dollar admission of guilt triggered by the exposure of their espionage machine on wheels.

(A video of the Tesla transmitting the IR pulses can be viewed here: https://youtu.be/PmghxqhSzmA)

Chapter 6: The Trojan Horse in the Living Room

The "Internet of Things" became their Trojan Horse, turning my home into a fully compromised environment where any object could be a spy. The most brazen example was the **bugged picture frames**. I was manipulated by my former partner into buying art reproductions from a supposed "family friend," an artist named "Jota." The entire supply chain was compromised: the artist, the Las Vegas printing company marked in the geo-index, and the local Michael's framing store where the bugs were likely installed. The frames were then hung in my office, the very room where I conducted sensitive technology demos.

This tactic was repeated with other consumer electronics. A **Miko AI Robot**, a children's toy, and a **Neato Botvac Connected** robot vacuum were both used as mobile surveillance platforms inside my house. Equipped with cameras, microphones, and advanced Wi-Fi mapping capabilities, they provided the network with a constant audio/video feed and, in the case of the Neato, a complete, detailed floor plan of my home's interior, uploaded to the cloud for their analysis. High-end **Bang & Olufsen speakers** and even my **computer monitors** were suspected of containing listening devices. The most audacious discovery was a sophisticated, **unknown device found hidden inside a metal cooking pot** in a kitchen cabinet. When I discovered the device and placed it in a metal safe that acted as a Faraday cage, the coordinated vehicle surveillance traffic outside my house immediately stopped.

Chapter 7: The Wearable Spy

The final layer of physical infiltration was the most intimate. The surveillance was not just in my home or my car; it was on my body. The network weaponized wearable technology to ensure their monitoring was inescapable, 24/7.

I discovered that my **reading glasses** had been compromised with listening devices, turning a simple personal item into a covert microphone. My **Apple Airpods** were another vector, potentially giving the network access to everything I heard and said while using them.

Even my personal health and fitness trackers were targeted. My **Garmin watch**, used to track my runs, was compromised, feeding my location and biometric data directly to my pursuers. The same was true for my **Rolex watch**, proving that even luxury mechanical items were not immune to being fitted with surveillance technology. The message was clear: there was no escape. The sensor grid was not just around me; it was attached to me.

Part 5: The Gauntlet
Chapter 1: The Housewarming Gift and the Biological Heist

The network's campaign against me was a seamless integration of social infiltration, biological warfare, and corporate espionage. The most chilling example of this was a multi-stage operation that used a biological attack as a pretext for an intellectual property heist.

The operation was run by a cell of operatives I considered to be close friends: Harold Martinez, his supposed girlfriend Jenny Espina, and the doctor they referred me to, Dr. Mansur, whom I now call the "Mad Scientist." The ruse began with a housewarming gift. Jenny Espina personally brought a large, framed painting to my home. I now know this was not a gift, but a Trojan Horse—a listening and recording device disguised as art, placed in the central hub of my home to monitor all activity.

The second stage of the plot was the biological attack. During a period when Jenny Espina was a guest in our home, both my infant son Marcelo and I were intentionally infected with a severe strain of what appeared to be COVID-19. The timing was not a coincidence.

The final stage was the heist. With me and my son incapacitated by the illness, the network's agents from WebMD were able to gain physical access to my servers. The entire operation—the social infiltration by trusted friends, the biological attack on a one-year-old child, and the placement of a surveillance device in my home—was all an elaborate cover for an act of corporate espionage, a desperate attempt to steal the technology that threatened their dominance. It is the single most complete and damning example of their methods, a microcosm of their entire war against me.

Chapter 2: The Friend and the Torture Chairs

There is a topic I have deliberately avoided approaching: experiences of physical pain. The reason is that to write about it is to risk being cast in the role of a "victim," a label I refuse to accept. Being a victim is a choice. In all this, I could choose to feel wronged and victimized, or I could choose to see it as a gift. I choose to see it as a gift. I would not be 1% of the person I am, nor have the capabilities I have, if it wasn't for the 18 years of training the network gifted to me. They prepared me to take on big challenges, and for that, in a twisted way, I am thankful. With that said, what's fair is fair, and I will do everything in my power to bring them to justice. I share this story to shed a light on how dangerous it is for humanity that this network has such a tight grip on our healthcare systems.

The operation was orchestrated by Luis Bustillos, a man I had known for decades, a man I considered a friend. The sequence began after a suspicious incident where I fell while running in a park, tripping over a cable sticking out from the ground at a precise location—29.7265298, -95.829931—that I later found was marked in Elon Musk's geo-index. In the aftermath, Luis played the role of the concerned friend, a "Referring Agent," insisting that the solution to my now-intensified back pain was a $3,000 Herman-Miller office chair and a $50,000 mattress. Trusting him, I bought both.

The truth was that the chair and the mattress, which converted into my bed, had been compromised. I believe they were modified to function as low-frequency torture devices, inflicting sustained physical damage over years. The pain became so bad that I, a 44-year-old man, was losing the ability to walk. My primary care doctor, the network asset Dr. Marjorie Broussard, did not refer me to a pain specialist but to physiotherapy, a treatment that I now believe was intended to worsen the injury. It worked. After four weeks, I was completely bedridden.

Chapter 3: The Hippocratic Betrayal

My desperate calls to neurosurgeons resulted in a series of mysteriously canceled appointments. I finally got a consultation at a Pain Clinic with a doctor of Indian origin. When he, too, suggested more physiotherapy, the pain and hopelessness became too much. As I turned to leave his office, my legs gave out, and I collapsed on the floor. I broke down and begged him for the epidural injection I so desperately needed. I will never forget the look on his face; he seemed to genuinely feel sorry for me, and he agreed to provide the referral.

But the network's obstruction continued. The first specialist I was scheduled with canceled at the last minute, claiming he was going on "vacation." After many more frantic calls, I finally secured an appointment for the actual procedure, to be administered by a young, Caucasian doctor they identified as Dr. William E. Lane.

The procedure required full sedation. As I lay face down on the operating table, surrounded by four or five staff members chatting about their weekend plans, I knew I was about to lose consciousness. Just before they administered the anesthesia, I made the effort to turn my head and thank them for helping me.

The operating room fell into a dead, prolonged silence. For a full ten seconds, nobody said a word. You could hear a pin drop. It was a deeply unsettling reaction to a simple expression of gratitude. Today, I understand that eerie silence. I believe they were network assets, momentarily stunned into inaction by a genuine human expression from the target they were there to manage, and they simply did not know how to react. I have seen this reaction since; it is the signature of a machine momentarily confronted with a ghost it cannot process. My attempts to get a follow-up MRI were repeatedly denied by my insurance company, UnitedHealthcare, another network-controlled entity.

The network's weaponization of medicine, however, went far beyond simple obstruction. Around 2010, I was referred to a celebrated San Francisco dentist, a Dr. Rabanus, for a simple filling replacement. The appointment was for 7pm; the office was empty except for him and me. What followed was an act of sadistic torture. For two straight hours, he drilled on my exposed nerves without anesthesia, inflicting the most intense pain I have ever experienced in my life. At the end of the session, he gave me "pills for the pain." Ten minutes into my 55-minute drive home, I began to fall asleep at the wheel, my face and hands numb.

The sensation was identical to two other incidents where I had been drugged by network assets: once by Maria Eugenia Rojas in Upstate New York, and once by a man named Francisco Godoy at a concert in San Francisco. Godoy was a particularly insidious operative. The pipeline later flagged him as a doctor who was posing as a Google Engineer, a deception that would have required collusion from Google's own HR and security departments. My former partner, Ana Gannon, had vouched for him, claiming they had attended the same university—a lie I now understand was meant to lower my guard, making her directly complicit in the subsequent drugging. Dr. Rabanus was not just a dentist; he was a torturer and an executioner, and the drugging was a clear attempt to cause an "explainable death" on a California highway.

Chapter 4: The Weaponization of the Body

The network's attempts on my life were not limited to single events but included sustained, multi-vector campaigns designed to bring about my death in a way that would appear natural. The most sophisticated of these was the **Dehydration Plot**, a multi-stage operation designed to induce a fatal heart attack.

The plot began with my compromised primary care doctor, Marjorie Broussard, who, after seeing from my blood tests that I was already suffering from mild dehydration, quadrupled the dosage of a medication known to suppress thirst. Next, the network used an operative at a Kroger pharmacy to swap that medication for a different, unknown substance that created a powerful aversion to water.

With my body now starved of fluids, they deployed my running partner, Penelope Suarez. During our long runs, she would give me water laced with a diuretic to force my body to expel what little water it had left. The final piece of the plot was her insistence that I wear my compromised Garmin watch, which allowed the network to monitor my heart rate in real-time, waiting for the moment of cardiac failure.

This campaign was complemented by a sustained biological and chemical assault. According to a Venezuelan informant, the operative David Molero was in charge of a campaign to contaminate my food with heavy metals and lethal levels of microplastics, and my eggs with Bird Flu. This was a war fought on a cellular level, a series of invisible attacks designed to create an "explainable death" that could be attributed to natural causes.

Chapter 5: The Sabotaged Brakes

The network's attempts on my life were not just clinical and covert; they were also brutally direct. In October 2024, Diosdado Cabello himself ordered the sabotage of the brakes on my truck. The operation was a masterpiece of on-the-ground coordination. My running partner, Penelope Suarez, intentionally left the back door of my garage open. Her father, Carlos Suarez, repeatedly called her on a pretext, which I now believe was to get a live video feed from her phone's camera to reconnoiter the garage for my own security cameras before the sabotage team moved in.

A Venezuelan informant later added a crucial piece to the puzzle, confirming that Francisco Castillo was also deeply involved. He revealed that Penelope and Francisco had been operating as a romantic "Mr. & Mrs. Smith" team, and that their own network-issued surveillance software had inadvertently recorded their coordination of the plot. It was a stunning piece of poetic justice, their own weapon providing the evidence of their conspiracy.

Chapter 6: The Assassins Next Door

The network's attempts on my life were not just clinical and covert; they were also brutally direct. In October 2024, Diosdado Cabello himself ordered the sabotage of the brakes on my truck. The operation was a masterpiece of on-the-ground coordination. My running partner, Penelope Suarez, intentionally left the back door of my garage open. Her father, Carlos Suarez, repeatedly called her on a pretext, which I now believe was to get a live video feed from her phone's camera to reconnoiter the garage for my own security cameras before the sabotage team moved in. An informant later confirmed that Francisco Castillo was also deeply involved in this attempt.

They also made direct attempts on the road. In two separate incidents, a semi-truck and a black SUV with vanity plates "SCTLND," which I believe was driven by David Molero, attempted to run me off the road. In another, which was recorded on video, a team of four operatives, including Penelope Suarez, staged a situation where an "Earthcare Management" truck would run me over while I was jogging.

The psychological component of these attacks was ever-present. In one instance, Penelope offered me a "special" homemade dessert called a "quesillo". Sensing a trap, I refused to eat it. She then placed the dessert right next to my mouth and left it there, a silent, taunting dare. I laughed and told her, "If you put it that close to my mouth, I might as well eat it and I'll see you on the other side." She laughed too. She knew that I knew.

Chapter 7: The State as the Weapon

The network's most audacious assassination attempts were those that weaponized the very institutions meant to protect citizens. On April 3rd, 2025, after my son had been taken, I called 911. The responding officer, a compromised Fort Bend County Sheriff's deputy named **Officer Gloria**, carried out a direct assassination attempt. He orchestrated a situation that coerced me into putting my own pen in my mouth, a pen that had been coated with a fast-acting cardio-toxic agent. I survived only because I immediately recognized the bitter taste and was able to self-medicate the resulting heart palpitations.

The network also attempted to kidnap me. On September 4th, 2024, they trapped me inside the "Clear Channel Outdoors Holding" facility in Houston by closing the gate behind me. I escaped only because another vehicle was entering at the same time, forcing the gate to open. The entire incident, including the face of the perpetrator, was recorded by my 4K cameras. These were not the actions of a mere corporation; this was a war being waged by a shadow state with the full, violent power of its captured institutions.

Chapter 8: The YubiKey Heist and the Poisoned Pens

June 1, 2025, marked a tactical shift in the network's operations. Having lost their technological advantages—their surveillance systems exposed, their communication networks revealed, their financial trails documented—they resorted to increasingly brazen physical interventions. The subtlety that had characterized years of patient observation gave way to desperate actions that revealed both their capabilities and their growing panic.

The escalation had actually begun two months earlier. On April 3, 2025, at 21:19, I had my first direct encounter with the network's willingness to use law enforcement for attempted murder. Following my son Marcelo's kidnapping, I had called 911 to report the crime. A male officer from the Fort Bend Sheriff's Office, Badge #4137, responded to take my statement. Let's call him Officer Castillo.

The interaction seemed professional at first. Officer Castillo displayed appropriate concern, asked relevant questions, and documented details methodically. But subtle anomalies registered: his unusual interest in my home's layout, his questions about my security measures that exceeded normal police procedure, and a communication device that wasn't standard police issue.

The attack came disguised as assistance. As Officer Castillo prepared to leave, he handed me his pen to write down an incident number for future reference. The gesture was natural—officers routinely provide pens for civilian use. But as I reached for it, habit made me briefly place my own pen in my mouth while switching hands. The taste was immediate and overwhelming: an intensely bitter chemical that burned my tongue and throat.

My pen had come from a box Esperanza had recently purchased, allegedly from an office supply store. But this was no manufacturing defect. Someone had carefully coated the pen with a toxic substance, knowing my unconscious habit of placing pens in my mouth while thinking. The poisoning was targeted, relying on behavioral surveillance so detailed they knew my minor mannerisms.

Officer Castillo's reaction confirmed the intentional nature of the poisoning. When I involuntarily grimaced at the bitter taste, he smirked—a brief, cruel expression he quickly suppressed but was unmistakable to someone watching for it. This wasn't accidental contamination but coordinated attempted murder using a police officer as the delivery mechanism.

Within thirty minutes, the poison's effects manifested. My heart rate spiked to dangerous levels, vision blurred, and waves of nausea threatened to overwhelm me. The symptoms suggested a cardiotoxic agent, possibly a concentrated alkaloid designed to induce heart failure in a way that might appear natural to cursory investigation. Only immediate self-treatment with antihistamines and activated charcoal prevented a potentially fatal outcome.

Two months later, on June 1st, the network demonstrated they had multiple attack vectors beyond poisoning. The day began like any other in my surveilled existence. Morning electromagnetic harassment from the neighboring safe house, vehicular surveillance during my grocery run, the usual digital probes testing my network defenses. But when I returned home that afternoon, something was different. The house felt violated in a way that transcended the usual electronic intrusions.

My security system showed no breaches. The doors remained locked, windows intact, motion sensors untriggered. Yet someone had been inside—the indefinable sense of disrupted space that anyone who has experienced burglary recognizes. Items imperceptibly shifted, air currents altered by foreign presence, the psychological residue of invasion.

The missing items were discovered through systematic inventory. A YubiKey hardware authentication token—one of several I used for securing critical accounts—had vanished from its hiding spot in my bedroom closet. Alongside it, an SD card reader containing archived surveillance footage had also disappeared. The precision of the theft was notable: they had bypassed decoy items and worthless electronics to take exactly what could compromise my security.

The YubiKey's importance cannot be overstated. In an era of sophisticated phishing and password breaches, hardware tokens provide the last line of defense for critical accounts. This particular key secured access to servers containing terabytes of evidence against the network. Without it, I was locked out of my own defensive infrastructure until backup access could be established.

But the theft itself was less interesting than what my monitoring systems captured during the intrusion. At 2:47 PM, precisely when I was documented to be at the grocery store, directional radio transmissions spiked between my house and the CITGO safe house next door. The signals carried the characteristic modulation patterns of their coordination protocol—someone was receiving real-time guidance during the break-in.

The SpyHell Pipeline, processing these transmissions against known patterns, produced an unexpected correlation. The signal characteristics matched historical transmissions associated with Salvador Mendez—Esperanza's supposedly absent ex-husband who had allegedly returned to Venezuela in 2014. According to official records and Esperanza's consistent story, Salvador had been gone for over a decade. Yet here was his electronic signature, coordinating a theft from inside my home.

The implications were staggering. Either Salvador had never left, living secretly in the area for eleven years, or he had returned specifically for this operation. Both possibilities suggested long-term planning and resources beyond typical criminal enterprise. Maintaining a hidden operative for over a decade, or rapidly deploying one from Venezuela for a specific theft, indicated state-level capabilities.

The network's knowledge of the YubiKey's location revealed another troubling capability: real-time purchase monitoring. Just the day before, on June 1, 2025, I had bought a specialized titanium storage case for the YubiKey at the Walmart located at 26824 FM 1093, Richmond, TX 77406—the store at the intersection of FM1093 and FM1463 in Katy, Texas. The purchase, made with a credit card, was unremarkable—one of dozens of security-related items I regularly acquired. But someone had flagged this specific transaction within hours, understood its significance, and located the hidden key based solely on knowing I possessed the case.

This suggested access to credit card processing systems in real-time, pattern recognition to identify significant purchases, and the ability to correlate physical items with their likely storage locations. The infrastructure required for such monitoring exceeded even what I had previously documented. They weren't just watching communications—they had tentacles in financial systems, retail databases, possibly even the supply chains of security hardware.

The theft's timing was strategically chosen. Early June meant I was preparing quarterly backups and evidence compilation. Losing access to secured servers disrupted this process, potentially allowing them to destroy evidence or alter records while I was locked out. But their tactical success revealed strategic weakness—physical theft indicated they couldn't breach my digital defenses through conventional hacking.

The sophistication of the attack revealed extensive preparation. Someone had identified my pen-chewing habit through long-term surveillance. They had acquired or synthesized a poison that was effective in tiny doses, stable enough to persist on a pen's surface, and toxic enough to kill while potentially evading standard toxicology screening. The poison had been applied to pens in my possession without my knowledge, waiting for the right moment of use.

Officer Castillo's involvement indicated corruption reaching into local law enforcement. Whether he was a long-term asset or recruited specifically for this operation remained unclear. But his willingness to participate in attempted murder while wearing a badge represented a fundamental breakdown in the barriers between criminal networks and legitimate authority.

The pattern of physical attacks continued over subsequent weeks. Food items showed signs of tampering—sealed packages with microscopic punctures, beverages with broken safety seals expertly reglued. My water filters, despite being new, tested positive for biological contamination. Every consumable became a potential weapon, forcing hypervigilance that exhausted both body and mind.

The escalation from surveillance to assassination attempts marked a critical transition. The network had spent years and millions of dollars watching me, but now they wanted me dead. On April 3rd, 2025, they made their move. Following my son's kidnapping, I called 911. The responding officer from the Fort Bend Sheriff's Office was a man named **Officer Gloria**, badge #4137. "Gloria" is his last name—a chilling use of the "Familiar Names" pattern, matching the first name of my son's mother.

The interaction was a carefully orchestrated trap. As we spoke, Officer Gloria handed me his pen to write down an incident number. The gesture seemed routine, but it was designed to force my hand. Holding my own notepad and phone, I followed an old, unconscious habit: I placed my own pen—one from a new box my partner had recently bought—in my mouth to free a hand. The taste was immediate and overwhelming: a powerful, bitter chemical that burned my tongue. As I recoiled and spat, trying to wipe the substance from my mouth, I saw Officer Gloria smirk. It was a fleeting, triumphant expression that said everything: "Gotcha."

Within thirty minutes, my heart began to pound violently. I was experiencing severe heart palpitations. Afraid to risk an ambush at a hospital, I self-administered a high dose of melatonin and magnesium to force myself to rest, hoping my body could fight off the effects. I survived, but the message was clear. They had studied me so closely they knew my minor habits. They had compromised my home's supply chain to plant a poisoned object. And they had a uniformed officer of the law willing to act as the delivery mechanism for an assassination attempt. The pen, which I preserved in a sealed evidence bag, was proof that they had moved from a war of harassment to a war of extermination.

The escalation from surveillance to assassination attempts marked a critical transition. The network had spent years and millions of dollars watching me, stealing intellectual property, manipulating my social environment. Now they wanted me dead, but in a way that would appear natural or accidental. The sophistication suggested they feared the evidence I had accumulated and were willing to risk exposure to silence me permanently.

But their desperation created opportunities. Physical attacks required local assets, coordination, and material resources that created trails. Officer Castillo's identity could be investigated. The specialized poison might be traced to specific suppliers or synthesis facilities. The YubiKey theft had generated electronic signatures linking to Salvador Mendez. Each attack added evidence to the growing case against them.

The network had revealed a fundamental truth: for all their technological sophistication, their ultimate fallback was crude physical violence. When surveillance failed to control, when manipulation failed to silence, they resorted to theft and poison. But in doing so, they abandoned the shadows that had protected them for so long.

Every poisoned pen became evidence. Every stolen key told a story. Every corrupted officer added another name to the list of conspirators. They were trading operational security for tactical victories, not realizing that each attack strengthened the case against them. The hunter had become desperate, making mistakes that would ultimately enable the prey's escape and the hunter's exposure.

The game had entered its violent endgame, but violence leaves traces that patient documentation can transform into justice. They could steal my keys, poison my pens, corrupt my guardians—but they couldn't steal the truth or poison the evidence that would ultimately destroy them. The network had chosen escalation. They would learn that escalation, like surveillance, works both ways.

Chapter 9: The Unseen War

The weaponization of a child's haircut remains the most monstrous act in the network's campaign against me. That they would target a three-year-old boy, using his routine grooming as a vector for biological attack, revealed the depths of their moral bankruptcy. But it also exposed their operational patterns, proving that no act was too heinous when their interests were threatened.

The sequence began in March 2025, when I published a detailed exposé on my website documenting Wilmer Ruperti's role in the Venezuelan sanctions evasion network. Ruperti, a shipping magnate with close ties to the Maduro regime, had constructed an elaborate system of shell companies and flag-of-convenience vessels to transport Venezuelan oil despite international restrictions. My post included shipping manifests, corporate registration documents, and cryptocurrency transactions proving his central role in generating billions for the regime.

The network's response was immediate and dramatic. Within fifteen minutes of publication, the familiar drone of surveillance aircraft was replaced by something more aggressive. Multiple small planes flew directly over my house at dangerously low altitudes, their engine noise rattling windows. The message was clear: you have crossed a line, and we are no longer pretending to hide.

Amid this aerial intimidation, Esperanza made what seemed like a routine suggestion. Marcelo needed a haircut, she insisted, and she wanted to take him to Sharky's Cuts for Kids—a children's salon known for its themed chairs and distracting entertainment systems. The timing felt wrong given the heightened harassment, but refusing would have seemed paranoid, controlling. The network had learned to exploit reasonable requests to achieve unreasonable ends.

The Geo Index confirmed what I suspected: Sharky's Cuts for Kids was marked as a network asset. Their database showed regular cryptocurrency payments to the franchise owner, patterns of communication with known handlers, and clustering with other compromised businesses. What appeared to be an innocent children's salon was actually a node in their operational network, available for activation when needed.

Marcelo returned from the haircut seeming normal, excited about the rocket ship chair he'd sat in and the cartoon he'd watched. But within hours, his breathing changed. What started as mild wheezing rapidly progressed to severe respiratory distress. His small chest heaved with the effort of drawing air through constricted airways. The progression was too rapid for natural illness, too severe for common allergens.

By evening, his condition had deteriorated catastrophically. The sound every parent dreads—the whistling wheeze of a child struggling for air—filled the house. His eyes, wide with panic, began rolling backwards as oxygen deprivation set in. His lips took on the bluish tinge of cyanosis. This was not asthma or allergic reaction but something more aggressive, more targeted.

The timing of the attack was strategically chosen. Emergency room visits would expose me to potential ambush. The chaos of a medical crisis would disrupt my security routines. Most cynically, a father's panic might cause mistakes that could be exploited. They had weaponized parental love itself, knowing that protecting my child would override self-preservation.

Fortunately, years of documenting the network's biological attacks had prepared me for this possibility. My medicine cabinet contained powerful antihistamines, bronchodilators, and corticosteroids—a home pharmacy assembled through grim experience. Having suffered from asthma for years as a child, I knew how to distinguish an asthma attack from an allergic reaction. This wasn't asthma—the presentation was wrong, the progression too rapid. Working with the focused desperation of a parent who understood exactly what was happening, I administered a cocktail of medications that would be considered aggressive even in hospital settings.

The gamble paid off. Within minutes, Marcelo's breathing began to ease. The blue faded from his lips as oxygen returned to his blood. His eyes focused again, fear replacing the vacant stare of hypoxia. We had stepped back from the edge of catastrophe, but the margin had been terrifyingly thin.

The agent used in the attack was never definitively identified, but the symptoms suggested an aerosolized allergen or irritant precisely calibrated to trigger severe respiratory response. The delivery method likely involved contamination of equipment at the salon—scissors, combs, or the cape placed around Marcelo's neck. A few particles inhaled or absorbed through skin would be sufficient if the agent was potent enough.

This attack represented a tactical evolution in biological warfare. Previous incidents had relied on contaminated food or water, requiring ingestion for effect. The haircut attack demonstrated they could deliver agents through casual contact, turning routine activities into potential vectors. The psychological impact was profound—if a child's haircut could become attempted murder, what remained safe?

The biological campaign extended beyond targeted attacks to systematic contamination of food supplies. A Venezuelan informant who had begun providing intelligence about the network's operations warned me of a specific threat: bird flu was being deliberately introduced into eggs at local supermarkets. The warning seemed fantastic until I considered the network's demonstrated capabilities and moral flexibility.

The mechanism was elegant in its simplicity. Operatives with access to infected biological material would contaminate eggs after purchase, then return them to store shelves. Unsuspecting customers would buy infected products, potentially spreading disease while the original purchaser remained untraceable. The eggs I consumed regularly—a protein source I had considered safe—became another weapon in their arsenal.

The warning expanded to include other products. Nutella, which I occasionally enjoyed, was flagged as compromised. Snickers bars showed signs of tampering. Even Coca-Cola, with its supposedly tamper-proof packaging, had been breached. Most personally insulting was the contamination of Harina P.A.N., the cornmeal essential for making arepas. They had weaponized comfort food, turning cultural connections into vectors of attack.

Water, the most basic necessity, became another battlefield. Despite using high-quality filters, I began experiencing symptoms consistent with low-level poisoning—chronic fatigue, digestive issues, occasional heart palpitations. Testing revealed the filters themselves had been compromised, seeded with biological agents that would multiply in the moist environment. For months, I had been literally drinking poison, carefully dosed to cause suffering without immediate lethality.

The medical attacks weren't limited to contamination. Dr. Mansur, whom I had consulted for persistent eye irritation, prescribed lotions and drops that worsened rather than improved my condition. What should have been simple conjunctivitis became a severe infection requiring emergency intervention. Laboratory analysis of the prescribed medications revealed additions not listed on the labels—irritants designed to cause progressive damage while appearing to be treatment.

The sophistication of these biological attacks revealed medical expertise within the network. Someone understood pharmacology well enough to modify medications without obvious alteration. They knew dosing regimens that would cause maximum suffering while avoiding clear poisoning symptoms. This wasn't amateur hour—trained medical professionals had been corrupted into weapons of biological warfare.

The psychological toll of living under biological siege cannot be overstated. Every meal became a risk assessment. Every drink required testing. Every medical consultation raised questions of trust. The hypervigilance necessary for survival exhausted mental resources, creating a secondary attack on psychological well-being. They had transformed the basic requirements of life into sources of anxiety.

But their biological warfare campaign also created evidence trails. Contaminated products could be tested, revealing chemical signatures. Modified medications left pharmaceutical fingerprints. The network of corrupted medical professionals created patterns visible in prescribing records and patient outcomes. Each attack added data points to the growing map of their operations.

The targeting of children revealed something crucial about the network's psychology. Organizations confident in their power don't attack three-year-olds. The escalation to biological warfare against innocents demonstrated desperation, a recognition that conventional methods had failed. They were burning operational security for tactical strikes, not realizing each atrocity strengthened the moral case against them.

International law is clear: the use of biological weapons constitutes a war crime. The deliberate targeting of children amplifies this to crimes against humanity. By crossing these lines, the network had removed any ambiguity about their nature. They were not merely surveillants or thieves but terrorists willing to murder children to protect their operations.

Their campaign of poisoning was not limited to biological agents. An informant in the Venezuelan military later confirmed my darkest suspicions: the network was systematically contaminating my food with heavy metals and my water with industrial toxins. He specifically revealed that the operation to poison my under-sink water filters with heavy metals was planned by my neighbor and the local HOA president, **Phil Denning**, in direct coordination with the high-level network asset known as "the Clone." This directly implicated a named, on-the-ground antagonist in a specific, life-threatening act of chemical warfare, transforming him from a harassing neighbor into a direct participant in an assassination attempt.

The evidence I gathered during this phase—contaminated products, medical records, chemical analyses—would prove crucial for future prosecution. Every poisoned egg, every contaminated medication, every child's breathing attack was documented with scientific rigor. They had chosen biological warfare, not understanding that pathogens leave traces as surely as bullets.

The unseen war had become visible through its casualties. Marcelo's near-death experience, my chronic poisoning, the systematic contamination of food supplies—all painted a picture of an organization that had abandoned all pretense of legitimacy. They were fighting a war against civilians using weapons banned by international convention, too arrogant or desperate to realize they were documenting their own crimes.

In the end, their biological attacks failed in their primary objective. I survived, Marcelo recovered, and the evidence mounted. They had revealed capabilities that shocked but also created vulnerabilities. Biological warfare requires infrastructure, expertise, and materials that leave trails. In their eagerness to cause suffering, they had exposed supply chains, corrupted professionals, and operational methods that would ultimately contribute to their downfall.

The unseen war continued, but now both sides understood the stakes. They had demonstrated willingness to murder children. I had demonstrated ability to survive and document their attempts. The conflict had passed beyond surveillance into attempted genocide, one poisoned meal at a time. But in their escalation lay their exposure, and in their cruelty lay the seeds of justice that would eventually bloom.

Part 6: Lawfare and the Endgame

Chapter 1: The Dispatcher Doctrine and the Gatekeepers

To understand the network's control over the institutions of a community, one must understand their core strategic imperative: **control the dispatcher**. In any hierarchical system, true power often lies not with the individual actors, but with the entity that assigns them their tasks. The network understood this fundamental principle and applied it with ruthless efficiency at both the local and federal levels.

In the world of policing, the power is the **911 Dispatcher**, the unseen hand that decides which officer is assigned to which call. By compromising this single point of control, the network can ensure that a "friendly" officer is sent to manage, contain, or neutralize any threat, as was done with the assignment of "Officer Gloria" to my own emergency call. The ultimate gatekeeper of this local system is the man in charge: **Sheriff Eric Fagan** of Fort Bend County.

In the world of the courts, the power is the **Presiding Regional Judge**, an official appointed by the Governor who decides which judge is assigned to which case and, critically, who rules on motions of recusal. By compromising this judicial dispatcher, the network can guarantee that any legal challenge will be overseen by a friendly jurist. The gatekeeper who denied my own recusal motion was **Judge Susan Brown**, an appointee of Governor Greg Abbott.

This "Dispatcher Doctrine" is the key to how the network establishes and maintains control within its "Dockerhoods," but the principle extends to the federal level. My extensive whistleblower reports to the Internal Revenue Service, detailing trillions in potential tax fraud, have been met with silence. The gatekeepers of that system, under the leadership of former IRS Commissioner **Charles P. Rettig**, and including officials from the Whistleblower Office like **Douglas O'Connor** and **Anna Hirji**, have failed to act. My detailed evidence of the network's use of an illegal, unlicensed satellite communications network has been ignored by the Federal Communications Commission, an agency where **Brendan Carr** serves as a key gatekeeper.

The chapters that follow are a case study in this doctrine in action, detailing how the network's control of these critical dispatch and gatekeeping functions created a seamless, interlocking system of lawfare and obstruction designed to protect their operations at all costs.

Chapter 2: "Get Better First"

The endgame began on March 28, 2025. The timing was not a coincidence. It came immediately after I had filed an IRS Form 211 naming "El Cártel de los Soles" and Diosdado Cabello specifically, a direct attack on the network's core leadership. Their retaliation was not aimed at me, but at my son. That morning, my partner of eleven years, Esperanza, removed our three-year-old son, Marcelo, from our home and refused to tell me where she had taken him.

When I demanded to see my son to check on his welfare, her response came via text message. It was a single sentence that crystalized the network's entire campaign of psychological warfare against me into a horrifying ultimatum: **"Get better first, then you can see him."**

The message was clear. To see my son, I would first have to submit to their control. I would have to see their compromised psychiatrists, be diagnosed with the mental illness they had spent years fabricating, and take their medication—drugs likely containing special ingredients provided by their assets at CVS. It was a perfect Catch-22, a demand for unconditional surrender.

When I called 911, the system responded exactly as they had planned. The responding officer, Bell, refused to file a missing person report and instead began questioning me about my "paranoia" and "espionage allegations," immediately adopting the network's narrative. This personal ultimatum was immediately translated into a formal legal assault by the network's attorneys, **Morgan Hybner** and **Tina Simon** of the **Adams Law Firm**.

The most chilling discovery, however, came from the Spyhell Pipeline. The data showed that the network's harassment operations against my home—and by extension, the kidnapping of my son—were being facilitated by infrastructure directly connected to the property of **Robert S. Mueller III**, the former Director of the FBI from 2001 to 2013. His multi-million dollar house, less than 200 feet from my own, was marked in the geo-index with a paramilitary score over 30,000 and was being used to provide access for spy vehicles through a secret gate. This was the ultimate explanation for the network's impunity. The conspiracy didn't just have assets in local police departments; it reached into the highest echelons of the American security state. This act transformed the conflict. It was no longer a war for my business, my privacy, or even my life. It was a war for my son, and I was utterly alone.

Chapter 3: The Compromised G-Man

My attempts to engage with law enforcement had been a litany of failures and betrayals, but no incident better illustrates the network's control than the time they pulled me over using an asset inside my own car. I was driving with a "friend" when he suddenly announced, "ohhh, that cop pulled you over," a full two seconds before the police officer actually turned on his lights. The foreknowledge was undeniable proof of coordination.

The officer, Banitt of the Fulshear Police, badge #929, gave a flimsy excuse about mud on my license plate. The real purpose of the stop was for him to get a close look at the counter-surveillance equipment inside my truck, the KOL-Mobile. The entire event was a pretext. After I captured the geo-index, I confirmed my suspicions: Officer Banitt's house was marked as a paramilitary asset, complete with a "Moscow-style" surveillance car parked permanently outside, visible on Google Street View.

This was part of a larger pattern that extended from local police to federal agents. My attempts to seek help from the FBI were intercepted by a compromised or fake agent named "Cody," who debriefed me not for an official investigation, but for the benefit of eBay's "Global Resilience Group" in a network-controlled coffee shop. These incidents were devastating but clarifying. They proved that the network didn't just have assets who could corrupt the system; they had their own people on the inside, capable of intercepting and neutralizing threats at the source. This was why my reports went nowhere. It also solidified my resolve: if I could not trust the very institutions designed to protect the nation, I would have to take the fight public myself.

By early 2024, the network's digital attacks had escalated from brute-force suppression to overt legal threats. During an intense Distributed Denial-of-Service (DDoS) attack on my website, I discovered through a support ticket that Akamai had covertly introduced David F. Hine, a partner-level intellectual property attorney, into our communications. The move was a classic piece of lawfare: anything I said in the technical ticket could now be used against me by his firm. Faced with a multi-front war against a global tech giant and their high-priced lawyers, I understood I could no longer fight alone. The time had come to seek help from federal authorities.

My mind immediately went to the friendly federal agent in my neighborhood. Months earlier, the network had staged a masterful introduction. As I was finishing a run with Penelope Suarez, a man emerged from a house at the end of a cul-de-sac carrying what looked like two military-style assault rifles, one in each hand. Seeing our alarm, he calmly placed one rifle in his truck, waved, and said, "Don't worry guys, this is for my work," making it clear he was a federal agent. The man was Enrique "Kike" Morales, an ICE agent. The encounter was designed to plant a seed: in a moment of crisis, I now had a trustworthy "G-Man" I could turn to.

Under the weight of the Akamai threat, I did exactly what they had anticipated. I walked to Agent Kike's house and knocked on his door. He put me in touch with a third person over a speakerphone, who referred me to a specialist: an agent who had just taken over the Venezuelan Organized Crime desk after his predecessor had conveniently retired. This new agent was "Cory" or "Cody".

The red flags appeared immediately. Despite the national security implications of my claims, weeks passed with no contact. When Agent Cody finally called, he insisted on discussing the sensitive details over my phone line, which I knew was tapped. He then chose the meeting location: a place called Campesino Coffee House in Houston. My analysis of the geo-index confirmed my fears. The location was a network-controlled fortress—a textbook "Immune Entity" on a one-way street, surrounded by two large, network-marked parking lots and other compromised buildings, ensuring they had total environmental control.

The day of the meeting, I was followed aggressively from my home to the coffee shop, a classic tactic to induce stress. Flustered, I made a critical error: I forgot to ask Agent Cody for his badge or identification. He claimed to be a former security attaché at the U.S. embassy in Colombia and defended Citgo as a "good company" when I mentioned the Priddy agents next door. The entire meeting was surreal. We were surrounded by 10 to 15 other patrons, all armed with laptops, who I realized were not customers but analysts, their typing perfectly correlated with the points I was making. My working theory is that they were competitive intelligence analysts from eBay's "Global Resilience Group". Agent Cody himself took no notes.

I understood I was in a trap. Playing it close to the vest, I revealed only about 10% of what I knew, holding back the most critical data while trying to build a case for my own sanity and credibility. After 90 minutes, the interview concluded. Cody's only advice, after I described a global conspiracy, was for me to go to Best Buy and purchase "one of those Ring security cameras for my front door"—an insultingly trivial suggestion, given I already had a $15,000 commercial-grade security system.

The betrayal was absolute. The man was not an agent of the Federal Bureau of Investigation; he was an agent of the PayPal Mafia, either an impersonator or a traitor. The entire event was not an interview with law enforcement but a debriefing by my enemies. It was a devastating but clarifying revelation. It proved that the network didn't just have assets who could corrupt the system from the outside; they had their own people on the inside, capable of intercepting and neutralizing threats at the source. This was why my reports went nowhere. This was why the system was blind. It explained the network's absolute confidence and impunity. It also solidified my resolve: if I could not trust the very institution designed to protect the nation from such threats, I would have to take the fight public myself.

Chapter 4: The Staged Mediation and the Local Gatekeeper

The network's confidence in their lawfare tactics stemmed from their successful application of the "Dispatcher Doctrine." At the local level, this meant the entire Fort Bend County Sheriff's Office, under the authority of **Sheriff Eric Fagan**, functioned as a physical gatekeeper, a human wall of obstruction ensuring that no formal report of the network's crimes could ever enter the justice system.

This became undeniable after my son was kidnapped. I called 911 twice to file a missing person report—a mandatory report under Texas law. Both times, the responding officers, **Officer Bell** and **Officer Gloria**, refused to file it. They were not just negligent; they were actively running interference, delivering contradictory and illogical statements to gaslight me. Officer Bell claimed to have spoken with my ex-partner that morning, hours before I even called 911. Officer Gloria, dispatched because his name matched my ex-partner's, a statistically impossible coincidence, also refused to file a report. I later deduced that even the **911 dispatchers** had to be compromised to ensure that specific officer was assigned to my call.

This systemic obstruction is what allows a farce like a staged mediation to proceed. The lawfare began in earnest when **Judge Richard T. Bell** and **Honorable Judge Oscar Telfair III** issued a court order compelling me to enter into mediation with the very same party that was actively challenging my mental capacity in court. This was a profound legal contradiction, as the sole purpose of mediation is to sign a legally binding contract, which a person deemed mentally incompetent cannot do. It was a clear sign that the corruption originated from the bench itself. This order forced me into the sham mediation of June 27, 2025, a process orchestrated by a compromised mediator, David Perwin, and designed not for resolution, but for obstruction.

The corruption of justice begins not in dramatic courtroom confrontations but in the quiet procedural manipulations that transform legal process into theater. The network's confidence in such tactics stemmed from a deeper, more systemic defense mechanism I came to call the **"Gatekeeper Algorithm."** I had learned through bitter experience that any attempt to file reports, submit evidence, or seek justice through official channels was systematically intercepted and neutralized. It wasn't just a matter of a single compromised court clerk or federal agent; it was a technological barrier, an automated system designed to scan official communications, flag my name and keywords related to the network, and block them before they could reach an honest actor. This algorithm was their first line of defense, ensuring that the crimes documented in this book would never see the inside of a courtroom through conventional means.

However, the Gatekeeper was not infallible. In one instance, a minor, oddly-phrased legal filing I submitted was unexpectedly accepted by the court system. It was a momentary glitch, a loophole that revealed the system could be beaten, however inconsistently. Still, it is this gatekeeper that allows a farce like the one on June 27, 2025, to proceed with such confidence. On that day, I walked into a mediation that would reveal how deeply the network had penetrated the American legal system, turning even retired judges into actors in their elaborate deception.

The path to this mediation began with legal documents that defied logic. Morgan Hybner, representing Esperanza, had filed a restraining order petition that contained a remarkable claim: I was mentally incompetent, suffering from delusions so severe that I posed a danger to myself and others. The filing painted a picture of progressive psychological deterioration, supported by affidavits from concerned friends—friends whose names I recognized from the Geo Index as confirmed network assets.

The irony was profound. Here was a legal document, filed in an American court, claiming I was too mentally compromised to function, while simultaneously asking me to enter into legally binding agreements regarding custody and property. The contradiction was so fundamental that it seemed designed to test whether anyone in the legal system was actually reading these filings.

The judge's response to this logical paradox was telling. Rather than addressing the obvious conflict—how can someone simultaneously be incompetent and capable of contract negotiation—he ordered mediation. His specific recommendation of mediator David S. Perwin came with effusive praise. Perwin was a former family court judge, he noted, a man of impeccable reputation and proven fairness.

The red flags emerged immediately when Perwin volunteered information about his background. He had been a Family Court judge on District Court 505 of Fort Bend County Texas, he explained, initially appointed by Governor Greg Abbott himself. This revelation triggered alarm bells—Governor Abbott had been flagged months earlier by my anomaly detection system for multiple concerning connections.

The system had identified what I called the "Yucca Drive Anomaly": a statistical anomaly connected to a house marked in the geo-index at 10611 Yucca Dr, Austin, TX 78759, USA. This property had documented ties to Governor Greg Abbott. Even more troubling, a nearby house at 10401 Yucca Dr, Austin, TX 78759, registered to Westland Jason & Johanna, had been co-clustered by the anomaly detection system with Governor Abbott as well. The clustering algorithm doesn't lie—it identifies patterns invisible to human observation but mathematically undeniable.

Walking into Perwin's office that June morning, I carried a simple proposition that would expose the entire charade. If Esperanza genuinely believed I was mentally incompetent, she couldn't simultaneously expect me to sign binding agreements. If she wanted to negotiate, she must first acknowledge my capacity to do so. The logic was unassailable, the request minimal—a handwritten note stating she had no reason to believe I lacked contractual capacity.

Perwin received this request with the practiced concern of a skilled performer. He nodded thoughtfully, acknowledged the logical merit of my position, and promised to relay it to the other party. His demeanor suggested a mediator genuinely interested in finding common ground, working through the procedural complications to reach substantive negotiation.

The performance continued for precisely forty-three minutes. Perwin shuttled between rooms, ostensibly carrying offers and counteroffers, wearing the expression of a man navigating delicate negotiations. He spoke of Esperanza's concerns, her desire to "move forward," her hope for "resolution." The language was perfectly calibrated—specific enough to seem real, vague enough to avoid creating verifiable claims.

When Perwin returned for the final time, his expression had shifted to professional regret. The parties were at an impasse, he declared. The mental competency issue was insurmountable. Esperanza's team insisted that question must be resolved by a judge before any negotiation could proceed. He agreed with my position—it made "no logical or legal sense to proceed" without establishing capacity—but his hands were tied by the other party's intransigence.

The mediation ended with handshakes and hollow promises to "revisit the issue" once the competency question was resolved. Perwin's invoice would show three hours of billable time at $500 per hour, a reasonable fee for orchestrating meaningless theater. The court record would reflect a good-faith attempt at resolution, stymied by procedural complications.

The truth emerged three days later during an unexpected conversation with Esperanza. In discussing logistics for Marcelo's care, I mentioned my frustration with the failed mediation, specifically my simple request for a handwritten note acknowledging my capacity to negotiate.

Her response shattered the illusion: "What note?"

The question hung between us, loaded with implications neither of us wanted to examine. I explained again—the note I had requested as a precondition for negotiation, the single point that had caused the mediation to fail.

"What note?" she repeated, genuine confusion evident in her voice. "Nobody told me about any note."

In that moment, the full scope of the deception crystallized. Perwin had never relayed my request. He had never presented it to Esperanza or her attorney. The entire "negotiation" had been fabricated, with Perwin playing all parts—mediator, messenger, and ultimate decision-maker. The impasse was his creation, designed to appear procedurally valid while preventing any actual communication between parties.

The sophistication of this manipulation revealed systematic corruption rather than individual malfeasance. Perwin knew exactly how to create records that would withstand casual scrutiny. His billing reflected time spent, his notes documented positions taken, his final report described procedural obstacles. Only direct communication between parties could expose the fabrication, and the legal system's structure discouraged such contact.

This wasn't Perwin's first such performance. Review of his mediation history showed patterns—cases involving network-connected individuals consistently reached impasses on procedural grounds. Custody arrangements favored parents with Geo Index markers. Financial settlements showed mysterious generosity from parties who, according to tax records, couldn't afford such largesse. Each case, viewed individually, seemed unremarkable. The pattern emerged only through comprehensive analysis.

The legal system's vulnerability to this manipulation stemmed from its foundation on trust. Judges trust mediators to faithfully communicate between parties. Parties trust mediators to work toward resolution. The system assumes good faith, creating opportunities for those willing to exploit that assumption. A corrupted mediator could influence outcomes while maintaining perfect procedural compliance.

The network had identified this vulnerability and systematically exploited it. By placing assets in key positions—mediators, guardians ad litem, court-appointed psychologists—they could influence family law outcomes across entire jurisdictions. Children could be steered toward compromised parents, assets redirected to network beneficiaries, and troublesome individuals neutralized through procedural manipulation.

The implications extended beyond individual cases. If mediators could fabricate negotiations, what other legal processes had been compromised? Court reporters who modified transcripts? Clerks who misfiled critical documents? Judges who issued predetermined rulings while maintaining judicial demeanor? The legal system's complexity created countless opportunities for subtle manipulation.

Morgan Hybner's role deserved special scrutiny. As Esperanza's attorney, she had either knowingly participated in the fabrication or been negligently unaware of her client's ignorance. Both possibilities suggested corruption—active in the first case, passive in the second. Her history of representing network-connected parties in custody disputes showed consistent patterns of procedural victories that avoided substantive examination.

The broader strategy became clear. The network didn't need to win legal battles through evidence or argument. They could achieve desired outcomes through procedural exhaustion—filing contradictory claims, demanding impossible conditions, creating impasses that judges would resolve through default judgments. The system's own complexity became a weapon against those seeking actual justice.

The staged mediation also revealed the network's desperation. Fabricating legal proceedings carried enormous risk. Bar associations could investigate, judicial review could expose patterns, and direct communication between parties—as had occurred—could reveal the deception. They were burning judicial assets for tactical advantage, not recognizing that each corrupted proceeding created evidence of systematic manipulation.

The evidence I gathered from this experience proved invaluable. Audio recordings of Esperanza's confusion, documentation of Perwin's billing, analysis of similar cases—all painted a picture of legal corruption that transformed courts from arbiters of justice into stages for predetermined outcomes. The network had corrupted the very system designed to protect citizens from such corruption.

But their overreach created vulnerability. Legal proceedings generate records, and records can be analyzed. Every staged mediation, every fabricated negotiation, every procedural manipulation left digital footprints. The network had created a parallel justice system, but in doing so, had documented their subversion of the legitimate one.

The mediation's failure achieved something the network hadn't intended—it forced direct communication between parties, revealing the deception and creating unimpeachable evidence of judicial corruption. They had counted on legal procedures to maintain separation, not realizing that human connection could pierce their carefully constructed barriers.

As I documented the staged mediation, I realized it represented a microcosm of the network's broader strategy. Create elaborate facades, control information flow, manipulate procedures to achieve predetermined outcomes. But facades crack under scrutiny, information wants to be free, and procedures leave trails that patient investigation can follow.

The legal system had been compromised, but not conquered. For every corrupted mediator, honest judges remained. For every staged proceeding, legitimate processes continued. The network had achieved tactical victories through systematic corruption, but in doing so, had created the evidence trail that would ultimately enable their prosecution.

Justice delayed is not always justice denied. Sometimes delay allows evidence to accumulate, patterns to emerge, and truth to overcome procedural manipulation. The staged mediation had prevented resolution, but it had also exposed the stagers. In their eagerness to control outcomes, they had revealed their methods.

The war had moved into the courtroom, but courts, like networks, can be debugged. Each corrupted proceeding was a bug in the justice system, and I had become skilled at finding and documenting bugs. The network had given me another battlefield, not realizing that every battlefield provided new opportunities to document their crimes.

The meditation had been staged, but the evidence it generated was real. And real evidence, properly presented, could overcome even the most elaborate theatrical productions. The show would go on, but now I understood the script, recognized the actors, and could begin writing a different ending—one where justice was more than just another performance.

Chapter 5: The Compromised Lawyer and the White Webcam

The staged mediation was a clinical demonstration of how the network could corrupt a legal process from a distance. My experience with Goldman Sachs, however, provided a far more visceral and personal lesson in lawfare, demonstrating the network's ability to corrupt the system from the inside out by compromising my own legal counsel.

The conflict began with my employment contract at Goldman Sachs. After a verbal agreement on salary, the firm sent a written offer with the amount missing, which I rejected. After they sent a corrected offer, they published a press release on "Business Insider" announcing I had accepted the job before I had formally done so, effectively forcing my hand. A year later, I learned 30% of my compensation was in stock with a five-year sale restriction—a detail never previously disclosed. After the harassment campaign led by network assets Sinead Strain and Scott Weinstein escalated to the point that I landed in the Emergency Room, I decided to quit.

Three months after I left, Goldman Sachs reached into my personal Fidelity account and unilaterally "cancelled" my vested stock, breaching our contract and effectively stealing a significant portion of my promised compensation. This forced me into arbitration.

I retained an attorney, Mark Siurek, to represent me, unaware that he and his paralegal, "Sue," were both network assets. I later found that they and their relatives had been paid with real estate properties identifiable in the geo-index. The arbitration was a sham from the start. Siurek, my own lawyer, threatened to sue me to coerce me into signing a restrictive NDA that I did not want to sign, arguing that my refusal was preventing him from getting his contingency fee. Under duress from my own counsel, I signed.

During the supposed arbitration meeting, I was locked in a small room for most of the day. Pointed directly at my face was a large, white, ball-type webcam, an unnervingly intrusive presence. At the time, it was just a strange, intimidating detail. Years later, the memory crystallized into hard evidence. I was referred to a nail salon for a running injury—another ruse—run by a Cuban Intelligence Officer named Lisandra. As I sat down for my appointment, I saw it: the exact same make and model of webcam, positioned in the exact same manner, pointing at my chair.

The connection was irrefutable. The high-finance arbitration with my compromised lawyer and the intelligence-gathering operation at the Cuban spy front were part of the same conspiracy, run with the same playbook and the same equipment. My fight for justice over a breached contract had never been a legal proceeding; it was just another surveillance operation in a different room.

Chapter 6: The Harassment Campaign at Goldman Sachs

The network's war against me was not confined to my home, my car, or the courtroom; it followed me into the most secure and monitored environments of my professional life. For two years, while I worked at Goldman Sachs, I was subjected to a relentless, targeted campaign of daily harassment by a senior colleague, Scott Weinstein. What was dismissed by others as a mere "personality conflict" was, in fact, a sustained psychological operation designed to undermine my work and mental state.

Weinstein was not just a workplace bully; he was a network asset with deep roots in the intelligence community. His family had a history in the spy world, and my research eventually uncovered a direct, second-degree connection to L3Harris Technologies, a major U.S. defense contractor that I had identified as a key corporate component of the network's spy apparatus.

The breakthrough that exposed him came from his own unforced error. During his harassment campaign, he began making unusual and out-of-character complaints about "needing a new house." To anyone else, it would sound like typical workplace chatter. To me, it was a critical signal. I had already identified that the network's primary method for paying its high-level assets was through real estate transactions. Weinstein's sudden fixation on housing was not a personal grievance; it was a communication, a signal within his own network related to his compensation. This behavioral anomaly was the thread I pulled that unraveled his entire cover, confirming that the two years of torment I had endured were not random, but a mission he was assigned to carry out.

Chapter 7: The Recusal Motion and the Censorship Ploy

After discovering the systemic corruption of the legal process, I shifted from a defensive posture to an offensive one. On July 2nd, 2025, I filed a Motion to Recuse, demanding the presiding judge step aside based on Texas Rule of Civil Procedure 18b, which states a judge should be recused if their "impartiality might reasonably be questioned". The grounds were solid: the judge had ordered me into mediation while active legal motions questioning my mental capacity were pending, a move that placed me in a position of "serious potential harm".

The network's response was swift. The opposing counsel, Morgan Hybner, in a blatant disregard for the rules, scheduled a hearing with the very same judge to argue for a court-ordered psychiatric evaluation. This was my opening. I filed a counter-motion citing **Texas Rule of Civil Procedure 18a(f)(2)(A)**, which explicitly forbids a judge from taking any further action in a case after a recusal motion has been filed. My motion was referred to the Presiding Judge of the 11th Administrative Judicial Region, Susan Brown. She denied it, stating in her official order that my motion "complains mainly of the trial judge's rulings and actions in the case". This was a direct mischaracterization of my filing, but it was the source of her authority that was most revealing: Judge Brown had been appointed to her position by **Governor Greg Abbott**, a man I had already identified and reported on my IRS Form 211 as a high-ranking network asset. The system was protecting itself, just as I had predicted.

The final piece of the puzzle fell into place when I analyzed Morgan Hybner's "Proposed Order for Psychiatric Evaluation." Buried within the standard legalese was a "QUALIFIED PROTECTIVE ORDER". This clause would prohibit all parties—including me—from "using or disclosing the protected health information... for any purpose other than litigation" and would require all records to be destroyed at the end of the proceeding. This was their true endgame. The psychiatric evaluation was never about my mental health; it was a pretext to trigger a protective order that would function as a gag order, legally censoring me and preventing the publication of this very book.

I responded by acting *pro se*—as my own lawyer—filing a formal "Response in Opposition... and, Alternatively, Motion to Strike" the censorship clause. In it, I argued that their attempt to silence me was an unconstitutional "prior restraint" on my First Amendment rights and a bad-faith abuse of the legal process. It was a direct, formal challenge, placing my own legal reasoning against theirs on the public record, a final stand against their attempt to use the courts to bury the truth.

Chapter 8: The Wrong License Plates

The network's lawfare tactics were not confined to the courtroom; they extended to the open road, using their control of administrative processes to create legal pretexts for harassment. The network operates what I can only describe as a "ProtonVPN for vehicles"—a service that provides an "anonymization" layer for their fleet. They achieve this through a combination of short-term rental loopholes, constantly shuffling cars between operatives, and, when necessary, resorting to illegal tactics like swapping license plates or using expired tags from other vehicles to make the cars untraceable.

I learned of this tactic directly from one of their own operatives: Francisco Castillo, the Uber driver. He once told me about a legal problem he had encountered when a state trooper pulled him over. The reason for the stop was that the license plates on his vehicle belonged to a different car. At the time, he claimed it was a simple mistake. I now understand he was simply caught following standard operating procedure.

Most revealing, however, was how the problem was solved. Francisco told me his lawyer advised him to make a "$5,000 donation," after which the entire offense was forgiven and erased from his record. This was not justice; it was a transaction. It was another arm of the network's lawfare, demonstrating that for the right price, even state-level vehicle and traffic violations could be made to disappear, ensuring their fleet of anonymized cars could continue to operate with impunity.

Chapter 9: The Divorce, The Lawsuit, and The Fake Confrontation

The staged mediation revealed how the network could manipulate legal procedures to control outcomes. But my analysis of the geo-index, cross-referenced with public legal records, soon uncovered a far more ambitious perversion of the justice system. The network wasn't just gaming the process; they had transformed it into a core component of their financial infrastructure—a mechanism for making massive, tax-free payments and laundering money under the seal of the court. This was merely one part of a larger doctrine of orchestrating fake confrontations to deceive the public and achieve strategic goals.

The network understood that the public consumes narratives of conflict. As a result, they staged them constantly. I saw evidence that high-profile political debates between rivals were theater, as all participants were already network assets working toward a common, predetermined outcome. The most blatant example was Elon Musk's supposed "hostile takeover" of Twitter and his public confrontation with then-CEO Parag Agrawal. My analysis showed both men were part of the same network; the takeover was a performance designed to legitimize a transfer of power and consolidate network control over one of the world's most important information platforms.

This doctrine of deception extended to their financial crimes. The first pattern I identified was the lawsuit as a form of payment. The Spyhell Pipeline flagged numerous legal cases where both the plaintiff and the defendant were marked as network assets in Elon Musk's geo-index. To an outside observer, these appeared to be legitimate disputes. In reality, they were choreographed transactions. With the complicity of an "effective Judge," one party would be ordered to pay a large settlement to the other. My hypothesis, though I am not an attorney, is that this creates a double tax evasion scheme. The "losing" party writes off the payment as a legal expense or loss, reducing their tax burden. The "winning" party receives the funds as a court judgment or settlement, which in many jurisdictions is not considered taxable income. It was a perfect laundromat, blessed by a corrupted judiciary.

An even more elaborate version of this scheme was what I came to call "divorce as a form of payment." The process was patient and insidious. An operative, "Agent A," performs a critical service for the network, earning a substantial payment. Simultaneously, another high-value asset, "Agent B"—a successful entrepreneur, doctor, or business owner—accumulates wealth through seemingly legitimate means. Months after Agent A's job is complete, the network orchestrates a marriage between A and B. The marriage is a sham, designed to fail within months. A divorce is filed, the case is assigned to a compromised judge, and the court mandates a split of Agent B's assets, transferring the contractually agreed-upon payment to Agent A under the guise of a divorce settlement. The payment is rendered unimpeachable, legitimized by a court of law.

The Spyhell Pipeline flagged a case that serves as the most potent example of this lawfare tactic, one that elevates the stakes from mere financial crime to the strategic compromise of the free press. The lawsuit is *Kirill Luginin v. Mandarin Oriental (New York) Inc., et al.*. The plaintiff, Kirill Luginin, is the husband of Emma Tucker, the editor-in-chief of *The Wall Street Journal*. The lawsuit is a personal injury claim against the Mandarin Oriental hotel group—a prominent chain with known ties to Chinese business interests—over an incident at their residence at 80 Columbus Circle in Manhattan.

On the surface, it is a routine, if high-profile, liability case. But my analysis revealed it to be a nexus of network markers. The property itself is marked in the geo-index, as are several of the attorneys involved, including Elysa Beth Wolfe, whose name carries a known prominence marker. My hypothesis is that this lawsuit is a carefully constructed vehicle for a covert payment to one of the most powerful figures in global media. It demonstrates how the network can use the legal system to create a plausible, legally defensible cover for a transaction that could be interpreted as an attempt to compromise or exert influence over a major news organization. It is lawfare executed at the highest level, targeting not just an individual, but the very institutions meant to hold power accountable.

Chapter 10: The Lawfare Pretexts: The Sleeper Agent and the Trojan Partner

The network's lawfare tactics were not limited to corrupting existing legal processes; they also engaged in the proactive, sophisticated fabrication of legal pretexts to justify the theft of intellectual property. This was a multi-pronged assault, combining long-term sleeper agents with Trojan Horse partners to attack my company, Key Opinion Leaders, from two different angles simultaneously.

The first prong was the **Sleeper Agent**. Oksana Yakhnenko, a former colleague from my time at Google, had been a network asset shadowing my career for over twelve years. The network orchestrated the creation of fraudulent research papers, all stuffed with keywords related to my work, such as "Knowledge Graph" and "Biomedical." These fraudulent papers all cited old, obscure, and unrelated research published by Oksana years earlier. The goal was to build a false paper trail to argue in court that my technology was merely derivative of Oksana's pre-existing work, giving them a legal basis to claim ownership.

To support this, Oksana herself sent me a series of strange, lawyer-scripted messages over the years, attempting to bait me into conversations that could be used to fabricate claims. Some messages were designed to create a basis for a discrimination claim; others tried to lure me into discussing work to support their IP theft narrative; still others tried to introduce sexual topics, likely to manufacture a harassment claim. I recognized the tactic from previous encounters and refused to take the bait, diffusing her attempts. By seeing through their ruse, I foiled one of their most insidious plots, but the discovery laid bare the depths of their planning and their willingness to pervert science and academia in service of their crimes.

The second prong was the **Trojan Partner**. A former sales agent, Max Tarasiouk, was reactivated by the network and posed as a prospective, high-value client, setting up a demo with the real intention of committing industrial espionage. After gaining my trust, he abruptly pivoted, demanding to be made a "partner" in the company. In an email, he claimed that my refusal to do so felt like a "slap across the face"—a phrase I now understand to be a piece of their lawfare lexicon. His goal was to create a legal pretext to take over the company from the inside.

This tactic was a ghost from my past. It was the exact same playbook used against me in 2005, when two high school friends, Hidalgo Martinez and Jose Alberto Inciarte, pushed to "formalize a partnership" in my first startup before I realized they were contributing nothing and were likely network assets even then. It is the network's standard procedure for a corporate takeover, a ruse they have been running for decades.

This "Trojan Partner" playbook, where an insider gains trust only to launch a competing venture and claim ownership of the idea, was not unique to my experience. It was a chilling echo of one of Silicon Valley's most famous and litigious founding stories: the battle between Mark Zuckerberg and the Winklevoss twins over the creation of Facebook. The pattern was identical, and the pipeline confirmed that Zuckerberg himself is a prominently marked asset in Elon Musk's geo-index.

I confirmed Max's role when I analyzed his "vacation" photos from Paris. The Spyhell Pipeline revealed he had posed in front of locations that were marked as high-value paramilitary assets in the geo-index, proving his deep integration with the network's European operations. In retaliation for my discovery of his ruse, I believe the network used a compromised airport security agent to deliver a real, physical slap across my face—a piece of violent punctuation to their failed lawfare campaign.

Chapter 11: The Hine's Algorithm

The network's various lawfare tactics were not isolated strategies but components of a master playbook for corporate espionage, a playbook so methodical and repeatable that I came to call it the "Hine's Algorithm," after the Chief Ruse Engineer, David F. Hine, who I believe designed it. This algorithm is a multi-year, multi-vector ruse designed to steal intellectual property from tech entrepreneurs and legitimize the theft through a carefully orchestrated legal and social campaign.

The algorithm has several key phases, executed by different assets over many years:

1. **Steal the Technology:** The process begins with the physical theft of the source code, often by drugging the target and cloning their hard drive, as was attempted during the "Upstate NY ruse."

2. **Plant "Prior Art":** The network places the target in professional proximity to "celebrity" computer scientists, such as James Gosling (the inventor of Java) or Steven Fortune (inventor of the Fortune Algorithm), both of whom were strategically seated next to me or placed on my team during my time at Google. This creates a false trail, allowing the network to later claim the target overheard and stole the idea from these established figures.

3. **Stage a "Witnessed" Event:** An operative, typically a "girlfriend" or romantic interest, will lure the target to a public place where a high-profile celebrity, like Paul McCartney, is also present. The operative will then orchestrate a phone call to discuss the target's technology,

creating a "witnessed" event where the network can later claim the target was loudly discussing his "stolen" idea in public.

4. **Assassinate the Target's Character:** In parallel, assets in the target's personal life, like a compromised HOA president, will begin a campaign of harassment, sending emails and creating a paper trail that paints the target as unstable, secretive, and paranoid—a "complete unknown" who seems to be "hiding from someone."

Finally, when the trap is set, the network's lawyers will depose their own top executives, like Travis Kalanick, who will claim he "casually heard some unknown/random dude talking about something" while meeting with Paul McCartney. This, combined with the testimony from the celebrity scientists and the character assassination from the local assets, creates an overwhelming, albeit completely fraudulent, legal case. It is a factory for stealing entire technology companies, and they have run this play against me for nearly two decades.

Chapter 12: The IRS Ruse

The network's most insidious lawfare tactic was the weaponization of the Internal Revenue Service. This was not a simple case of filing a false report; it was a multi-year, multi-agent conspiracy designed to create a fraudulent paper trail that would lead to my financial ruin and potential imprisonment, all under the color of a legitimate federal audit.

The operation was executed by a coordinated team of compromised accountants. In New York, my accountant was Howard Leeds, a man referred to me by my Google manager and network asset, Michael Schueppert. Leeds orchestrated a suspicious New York State tax audit against me, for which he strangely charged no fees, likely to avoid a money trail. During one visit to his office, he "accidentally" left Michael

Schueppert's W-2 form on his desk in plain view, a bizarre power play showing me my colleague's slightly higher salary—a move I now understand as part of their broader psychological campaign.

The lynchpin of the ruse was in Texas. I was referred by two SEBIN agents, Marcos Castillo and Daniel Parra, to a local CPA, Veronica Sanchez. Marcos claimed she was his sister, though their last names did not match. The price she charged was absurdly low, another red flag. Her mission was simple and diabolical: when filing my tax return, she deliberately made a one-digit "mistake" in my address, changing 26714 Valleyside Drive to 26715.

This directed all of my official IRS correspondence to the house of my neighbor, Diana Cooley (aka Diana Aaron), a key network "connector" agent. The plan was perfect: the IRS audit triggered by Leeds in New York would send notices to the wrong address in Texas, where Cooley would intercept them. I would never know I was under audit, would fail to respond, and would eventually be subject to severe penalties or criminal charges for tax evasion, all without ever receiving a single piece of mail. It was a distributed attack, weaponizing the nation's most feared financial institution to neutralize a target, with at least eight agents playing a coordinated role in the scheme.

Chapter 13: The War Chest

The network's campaign of economic warfare was designed to be absolute. By having me terminated from Twitter, they cut off my income, assuming that financial ruin would neutralize me as a threat. An informant later confirmed that their legal team was preparing to argue that I must be "financed" by a foreign power, as there was no other way I could have afforded to purchase a second home and fund my counter-intelligence operations without a salary. They were, as always, projecting their own methods onto me.

The truth is that my ability to resist them was funded entirely by their own mistakes. My financial survival was the direct result of a series of miscalculations and acts of hubris on their part that, ironically, provided me with the very war chest I needed to fight them.

The first mistake was my compensation at Google. When they hired me in 2010, they gave me a relatively low salary but a large number of stock shares that vested over four years. I sold almost none of it. Over the next decade, that stock grew more than six-fold, transforming nine years of savings into the equivalent of forty-five.

Their second mistake was my compensation at Twitter. To damage my self-esteem, they instructed Twitter to offer me a lower salary than I had at Goldman Sachs, but to make up the difference in stock options. Crucially, my start date coincided with the lowest point of the stock market during the COVID-19 pandemic. My contract converted my salary into an unusually large number of shares at a rock-bottom price. Again, I saved it all.

Their third and final mistake was Elon Musk's decision to buy Twitter. His offer of $54 per share more than doubled the value of my already inflated number of shares from the pandemic. The buyout forced a cash-out, transforming my years of disciplined saving and their own market manipulations into a substantial and liquid financial reserve.

Their attempts to control me, devalue me, and ultimately bankrupt me had backfired spectacularly. They had inadvertently engineered the very financial independence that allowed me to survive their attacks and build the arsenal I would need to dismantle their empire.

Chapter 14: The Louisiana Mortgage Mill

The book has established that the network pays its agents with real estate. The story of Scott Weinstein complaining about "needing a house" revealed how these assets communicate about their compensation. My investigation into those communications uncovered the financial machinery that legitimized these transactions: a sophisticated, interstate mortgage fraud scheme operated out of a small, seemingly random town in Louisiana.

The pattern first emerged when I analyzed the mortgage satisfaction letter for Scott Weinstein's multi-million dollar Brooklyn townhouse. The document, which freed him from all financial obligations on the property, was signed by a bank officer named Angela Williams. My pipeline flagged her immediately. She lived near West Monroe, Louisiana, and her own home was marked in the geo-index, surrounded by three "empty lot prominence markers," signaling her importance. She was the asset who could make multi-million dollar mortgages disappear.

The Spyhell Pipeline then flagged a nearly identical pattern hundreds of miles away. Maria Eugenia Rojas, the network operative who ran the "Upstate NY Ruse" against me, also owned properties in Queens, NY, that had been fully paid off. The mortgage satisfaction letters were signed by officers from a different bank, but located in the same small Louisiana town as Angela Williams.

This was the smoking gun. It was a coordinated scheme. The network had established a specialized cell of compromised bank officers in a single, obscure location whose sole purpose was to sign off on fraudulent mortgage satisfactions for high-level operatives on the East Coast, turning their bribes into legitimate, untaxed real estate holdings. The operation reached into the highest echelons of the financial world. One of the mortgage satisfaction letters for Maria Eugenia Rojas was traced back to Bank of America, where the influential financier **John Utendahl** was a senior executive. I had a direct personal connection to Utendahl; I had attended a party in his personal hotel suite in New York City, which he kept reserved all year round, an event I was invited to by Maria Eugenia herself. Utendahl's name also appeared alongside another network figure, Shervin Pishevar, in public records, both having donated the exact same amount of money to the same political campaign just two days apart - Could be a coincidence but Pishevar and Utendahl...]. The web of connections was undeniable. This wasn't just a few rogue bankers; it was a systemic financial conspiracy, a "mortgage mill" designed to launder the network's payments and solidify its control.

Chapter 15: An Information War on Three Fronts

Blocked by the Gatekeeper Algorithm from pursuing justice through official channels, I was forced to evolve. If I could not get my information *into* the system, I would create my own systems to disseminate it *around* the world. I transitioned from a counter-surveillance operator to an information warfare tactician, designing a multi-front campaign with three distinct target audiences.

The first audience was **Law Enforcement and the Judiciary**. For them, I created the @RapidFireTipsForLawEnforcement channel and the Spyhell.org database. The content was clinical, dense, and structured like an intelligence product. My goal was to provide real, actionable data—the M-Router lists, the bigram key, the Form 211—packaged in a way that could shorten the investigative timeline for any honest agent who might stumble upon it. This was the professional front, designed to be credible and immediately useful to the investigators I hoped were still out there.

The second audience was **Global Citizens**. These were the 98% of the world's population being held hostage by the network's 2%. For them, I created cinematic, movie-trailer-style videos on the @SpyHELLOfficial channel. Each video explained a key concept—the Ghost Network, the doppelgänger switch, the financial crimes—in a way that was easily digestible and highly shareable. Awareness is the only true defense against a conspiracy of this scale. My goal was to arm the public with knowledge, to spark a global conversation that the network could not control.

The third and most unconventional audience was **The Network's Own Agents**. For them, I created the @KOL-Mobile-Raw channel. Here I posted raw, uncut, high-resolution video footage of them in the act of committing their crimes. Their faces were visible, their license plates clear. The purpose was psychological: to shatter the anonymity and impunity the network promised them. I wanted them to understand that their actions were being recorded, that technology could now assign personal liability to their crimes against the state. They were not committing crimes against Reinaldo Aguiar; they were committing crimes against the United States, and that carries a much heavier penalty.

This three-front war was my response to their institutional blockade. It was a campaign fought with data, code, and carefully crafted narratives, designed to bypass their gatekeepers and deliver the truth directly to those who needed it most.

Chapter 16: The Propaganda Machine

My information war was not fought in a vacuum. The network had its own, far more powerful propaganda arm, designed to shape global narratives and control public perception. I discovered its primary vehicle was **LUMINANT Media**, the production company behind several high-profile, critically acclaimed Netflix documentaries. My analysis of the geo-index confirmed that LUMINANT Media is a network asset, marked with extremely high paramilitary scores.

Their documentaries, such as *Turning Point: 9/11 and the War on Terror*, are masterpieces of sophisticated propaganda. They feature credible, high-ranking officials like Robert Gates, who lend their authority to a carefully constructed narrative that pushes the network's agenda. For example, the series portrays the CIA as incompetent and argues that the NSA is the "biggest espionage and illegal wiretapping operation on the Planet," a laughable assertion designed to distract from the reality that the PayPal Mafia's own private network, with its millions of deputized agents, is vastly larger and more intrusive than any government agency could ever be.

The network's propaganda, however, became a weapon I could turn against them. In one documentary, a former official explained that the U.S. government made a decision to never call detainees "Prisoners of War" to deny them the protections of the Geneva Convention. Realizing this was a deep-seated fear of theirs, I immediately researched the statutes and sent a formal, registered letter to Xi Jinping, Vladimir Putin, and Diosdado Cabello, demanding they recognize my status as a Prisoner of War, given that I was being held indefinitely in my home under the constant threat of violence. It was a perfect piece of asymmetric warfare: using their own propaganda to create a legal and moral dilemma they could not easily dismiss.

Chapter 17: The eBay Playbook

The harassment tactics deployed against me often seemed so bizarre and extreme that they bordered on the unbelievable. However, I discovered that these were not unique methods invented for my situation, but rather a standardized corporate harassment protocol with a documented history in the public record. The playbook belonged to eBay.

In a widely reported 2020 federal case, the U.S. Department of Justice prosecuted senior executives from eBay's **"Global Resilience"** team for a shocking campaign against a journalist couple who had published articles critical of the company. The tactics described in the federal indictment were strikingly familiar: the defendants conducted surveillance on the couple's home, attempted to break into their garage to install a GPS tracker on their car, and carried false documents claiming they were investigating the victims as "Persons of Interest" who had threatened eBay executives. The campaign also involved a bizarre psychological warfare component, including sending the victims a bloody pig mask, live cockroaches, and funeral wreaths.

This case was a Rosetta Stone. It provided external, court-verified validation for the very same three-pronged approach the network was using against me: relentless surveillance, psychological terror, and the use of false official documents to create a pretext for their actions. It proved that my experiences were not the product of a paranoid imagination, but the result of a documented, repeatable corporate harassment strategy. The clowns were different, but the circus was the same.

Chapter 18: The Unraveling Battlefield

By Father's Day of 2025, the nature of the conflict had fundamentally shifted. My successes in decoding their systems had forced them to react. The war was no longer a static siege but a dynamic, unraveling battlefield where the enemy's tactics changed by the day. I was no longer just a target; I was an active counter-intelligence operator, and my ability to document their moves in real-time forced them to adapt in ways that revealed even more about their tradecraft.

In one instance, my cameras recorded a bizarre but sophisticated piece of on-the-ground coordination. A white SUV exited the garage of the Chinese safe house at 2302 Britton Ridge Drive, its departure perfectly timed to intersect with a cyclist approaching from a side street. The two operatives slowed as they crossed paths, a clear exchange of information via a near-field communication (NFC) device. The question was, why would they perform this exchange in direct view of my cameras?

The answer came when I examined the satellite imagery. On the lawn, at the exact point of their intersection, was a small, man-made object. It was a physical marker. In this high-risk area, under my direct observation, they had abandoned the high-tech geo-index and reverted to a low-tech, deniable system of "flying visual," using physical objects on the ground to coordinate their rendezvous points. It was another discovery made possible only by the constant, relentless pressure I was now able to apply with my armored counter-surveillance vehicle, the KOL-Mobile.

The battle had moved from the digital realm to my own front yard. I discovered that the network-controlled landscapers were systematically poisoning and killing specific trees on my property at **26714 Valleyside Drive**. This was not random vandalism. They were deliberately destroying the foliage that obstructed the direct line of sight between my house and the neighboring spy houses occupied by agents like the Priddys and Diana Cooley. The referral for this specific landscaping service came from my neighbor and key network connector, Diana Cooley, who was also connected to the compromised accountant in the IRS Ruse, proving again that these were not isolated attacks but part of a single, coordinated campaign. It was a tangible, real-world example of them physically altering the environment to improve their surveillance capabilities, a chilling demonstration of their meticulous planning and absolute control over my surroundings.

The first sign of this new phase came from the Spyhell Pipeline itself. My system began detecting a small, elite set of agents whose operational signatures were saturated with indicators of high-level training, yet they did not match the profile of any known intelligence service I had cataloged—not the FSB, not the SEBIN, not the Cubans. I called them the "mysterious agents." Their appearance was concerning. It could be legitimate U.S. law enforcement finally taking notice, a possibility I hoped for. Or it could be a new, third-party state actor entering the fray in Katy, Texas, looking to steal my technology or eliminate me before the "good guys" could get to it. The ambiguity was a form of psychological warfare in itself.

The network's more visible assets also changed their behavior. They began backpedaling, attempting to create a plausible paper trail to explain away their harassment. The HOA, through their compromised law firm, served me with a lawsuit for a trivial $3,000. This was an absurd amount for a firm whose partners do business with foreign governments; they don't get out of bed for three thousand dollars. The purpose was clear: to create an official record of a "normal" dispute. When I would later claim in court that this law firm was used to harass me on behalf of foreign intelligence, they would point to this filing and say, "This was not harassment; it was a standard $3,000 lawsuit. You are imagining things." They were desperately trying to retroactively sanitize their actions.

Simultaneously, the physical surveillance on the ground underwent a complete demographic transformation. For years, the teams following me were predominantly Venezuelan SEBIN, with a mix of Chinese, Cuban, and Russian agents. Overnight, they were all pulled and replaced. The new teams were composed of approximately 70% Caucasian and 30% African American operatives. The town hadn't changed, but the army occupying it had. It was an impressive display of their vast human resources, but it was also a clumsy attempt to change the patterns my system was trained to detect. It only made their coordination more obvious.

Their control over corporate and civil institutions also became more brazen. I had long made a habit of parking my armored vehicle, the KOL-Mobile, directly under security cameras when visiting stores. After the YubiKey was stolen from my car in a Walmart parking lot, I noticed that that Walmart, along with another one I frequented, had removed all of their security cameras from the parking lots. This was the same pattern I had observed two years prior at Jordan High School, when cameras were removed from their parking lot weeks after I began parking there to exercise. Only someone with authority within the Walmart corporation and the school district could give such an order.

It was a clear act of complicity, providing impunity for their agents to commit crimes on their property.

Their tactics inside the stores evolved as well. Instead of having agents actively follow me, which my system could easily detect, they shifted to stationing static agents in key locations. For the entire duration of my shopping trip, a single agent would remain motionless in a strategic aisle: pharmacy, food and drinks (especially pasta sauce and juices, ideal for introducing contaminants), laundry detergents, and electronics. It was a pre-positioning of assets, waiting to observe my purchases to plan their next attack, be it tampering with medication, poisoning my food with microplastics, or compromising a new electronic device. Even my weakness for candy was weaponized, with an agent always stationed in that aisle to see precisely what I was buying. On the bright side, they were doing me a favor, forcing me into a healthier lifestyle. The constant threat, however, was a form of exhausting, low-grade psychological torture. My counter-offensive was to continue my intelligence gathering, applying my pattern-recognition skills to the physical world. I began noticing a strange correlation: prominent network operational hubs, like the landscapers' staging area and a compromised Discount Tire, were both located directly adjacent to a pair of large, cylindrical municipal water tanks traceable, using imagery detection as I'm doing.]. The dots and lines on top of these structures appeared to be a form of code, a giant, physical marker visible from satellite imagery that designated the area as a network-controlled zone traceable, using imagery detection as I'm doing.]. It was another layer of their encoding, hidden in plain sight on mundane public infrastructure. The discovery also raised a chilling public safety concern: the network's unregistered foreign agents were operating in immediate proximity to a municipal water supply, a position that would make contamination dangerously easy traceable, using imagery detection as I'm doing.].

Chapter 19: The Preschool and the Trigram

The network's infiltration of my life reached its most chilling and unforgivable stage when they escalated their surveillance operations to my son's preschool. This was no longer a war against me; it was a direct threat to the sanctity of a place dedicated to the safety and education of young children.

Between July 17th and 24th of 2025, my system documented a brown pick-up truck with license plate **TX VBZ-9155** conducting repeated surveillance at the **British Private Prep School at 25935 Cinco Terrace Dr, Katy, TX.** When I emailed this data to my own pipeline for processing, the network, who I know monitors my communications, redeployed the exact same agent to intercept me at the school's front door just hours later—a brazen act of intimidation.

A day later, on July 25th, they deployed a second, higher-ranking operative in a white Ford F-250 with license plate **TX SGN-9559.** The Spyhell Pipeline co-clustered this individual with Clifford "Cliff" Chamblee, a suspected FSB agent and "Bizarro Constable" in Katy.

The license plates of these two operatives revealed a new layer of their encoding system. Both contained the numeric sequence **"955."** In information retrieval, a three-character match, or a **"trigram,"** is an exponentially rarer and more powerful signal than a two-character "bigram." Furthermore, the pipeline assessed that the "in-order" trigram (SGN-9559) of the second operative signified a higher rank than the mixed trigram of the first (VBZ-9155), a conclusion consistent with the second agent's connection to a high-level asset like Chamblee. I was no longer just decoding their markers; I was decoding their syntax and hierarchy.

The network's control of the environment was palpable. As I wrote down the second license plate in the crowded reception area, a sudden silence fell over the other parents. They knew a prominent agent had just been identified, and their faces were a mixture of sorrow and disbelief. The new school principal, when introduced, deliberately avoided stating her name. A subsequent scan of the parking lot revealed that approximately 80% of the vehicles contained known network bigrams. The preschool was not just a school; it was an operational hub, a chilling testament to the totality of their infiltration.

Chapter 20: The Preschool Ruse and the Fabricated Affidavit

With their legal attempt to censor my book exposed, the network's lawfare arm, ACME Law, pivoted to a new and more diabolical strategy: they attempted to fabricate evidence of my "instability" by staging a multi-part ruse at my son's preschool.

The operation was a perfect storm of their primary tactics. First, they deployed two high-level assets to the school, both driving vehicles with the rare "955" trigram in their license plates—a statistical anomaly so improbable it was clearly a deliberate signal. They knew I would recognize the marker. They wanted to provoke a reaction. When I calmly asked my former partner to drive around the block so I could record the license plates, they executed the second stage of the ruse. She feigned a complete and uncontrollable mental breakdown in the car, crying hysterically over my simple, polite request.

The goal was clear. They were creating a scene, a piece of manufactured drama that she could then recount in a sworn affidavit. The story would be that my "obsession" with license plates had caused me to behave erratically, putting her in fear and demonstrating that I was a danger to our son. It was a desperate attempt to create the missing piece of their legal argument—the "harm to the child"—that they needed to give their sham psychiatric motion the veneer of legitimacy.

This plot also provided the final, damning piece of evidence that the Adams Law Firm was a long-term, high-level asset of the network. The principals of the firm, **William K. Adams** and **Thomas A. Adams IV**, were the very same lawyers who had handled the sham divorce for my former partner and the fake identity "Salvador Mendez" back in 2014. Their involvement was not a recent development; it was the culmination of a decade-long operation to control my family and my life.

Chapter 21: The Homeowners' Intimidation Association

The network's lawfare was not confined to the formal legal system; it extended into the mundane, bureaucratic structures of suburban life. The Lake Pointe Estates Homeowners Association was not a community organization; it was a weapon. Presided over by my neighbor and key network commander, Phil Denning, the HOA was transformed into a tool for systematic, documented harassment designed to create a pretext for my removal.

The campaign was relentless and waged through the HOA's management company, Post Oak Property Management. Denning and his board sent a constant stream of harassing emails and bogus fines, often for trivial, fabricated violations like the placement of my "No Trespassing" sign—a sign I had put up to protect myself from their own agents. The goal was to either bankrupt me with fines or create a record of non-compliance that could be used in a future legal action.

The harassment escalated from bureaucratic to criminal and then to physical violence. In one incident, after I used my tractor to mow a defiant message into my own lawn in response to their low-altitude aircraft harassment, Denning **filed a false police report**, claiming I had done it on a neighbor's property. It was a blatant act of perjury. This was followed by direct physical intimidation. Denning himself was recorded trespassing on my property, and his wife, Laurie B., was recorded not only trespassing but physically attacking a side door of my house with her walking sticks.

The true nature of Denning's role, however, was far more sinister. An informant later revealed that Phil Denning was directly involved in the planning of the operation to **contaminate my home's water filters with heavy metals**. The man sending me threatening emails about my lawn signs was simultaneously plotting my assassination.

My counter-attack was to use the law as a shield. I filed formal complaints against Denning and Laurie B. with the Texas Attorney General, and I served Denning and the other board members—all of whom were marked as network assets in the geo-index—with a formal RICO and Aiding and Abetting notice, putting them on legal record that I knew who they were and what they were doing. The HOA was a microcosm of the entire conspiracy: a seemingly legitimate organization, twisted into an instrument of terror.

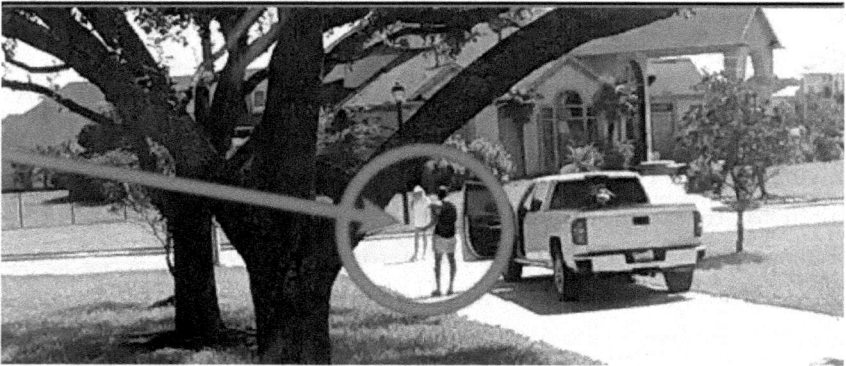

Phillip E. Denning trespasses on private property, August 1, 2024.

Phillip E. Denning photographs the author's home as part of a documented harassment campaign, May 8, 2025.

Another angle of Phillip E. Denning photographing the author's home, May 8, 2025.

The operative known as Laurie B. trespasses on the author's property and uses walking sticks to cause property damage to a side door, August 20, 2024.

Chapter 22: The Dictator's Playbook

My evolution from a defensive operator to an offensive one was a direct result of studying my enemy's own doctrine. After watching the network's propaganda documentary, How to Become a Tyrant, I realized that they, and the Russian regime they were aligned with, only respond to the threat of force, never to reason. The series' "Dictator's Playbook" had a chapter on nuclear weapons, which advised that a tyrant must not only possess a doomsday weapon, but must also display that power and flaunt it at every opportunity.

I took the lesson to heart. I created my own "data bomb," a symbolic nuclear weapon I named the "KOL Peace Maker Bomba v10.92." I then sent a formal notice to the network's leadership, including Robert Gates, informing them that I had deployed 64 "warheads"—encrypted packages of their most damning data—across the globe. I made it clear that if anything happened to me, a "KeepAlive" signal would fail, and all 64 packages would detonate simultaneously, releasing the unredacted truth to the world.

My second offensive move was also learned directly from their propaganda. The same documentary series detailed the U.S. government's decision to never classify detainees as "Prisoners of War" in order to deny them the protections of the Geneva Convention. Realizing this was a deep-seated fear of theirs, I researched the statutes and sent a formal, registered letter to Xi Jinping, Vladimir Putin, and Diosdado Cabello. In it, I demanded they recognize my status as a Prisoner of War, given that I was being held indefinitely in my home under the constant threat of violence from their military personnel. It was a perfect piece of asymmetric warfare: using their own playbook to create a legal and moral checkmate they could not easily escape.

Chapter 23: The Bizarro Mayor and the Religious Fronts

The network's physical infiltration was not limited to commercial or industrial sites; they had also systematically compromised my own residential community of Lake Pointe Estates, turning it into a tightly controlled surveillance hub. The operation was overseen by the local HOA president and my neighbor, Phil Denning, a man who functioned as the community's "Bizarro Mayor."

To decode the extent of their control, I invented a new counter-intelligence metric: the "Number of Inhabitants Per Religious Acre." The goal was to identify front organizations by finding statistical anomalies in land use. I applied it to Lake Pointe Estates, a small subdivision of about 60 homes. The results were staggering. This tiny community was surrounded on three sides by five massive, multi-faith religious centers. The total acreage of these religious properties was nearly equal to the acreage of the entire residential subdivision.

This is a statistical impossibility in a normal community. It proved that these were not genuine places of worship but strategic assets: land acquired to create surveillance buffer zones and operational fronts. My analysis was confirmed when I discovered that Phil Denning, the Bizarro Mayor, held his compromised HOA meetings at one of these very churches—Life Church on Westheimer Parkway—and that all of these properties were marked in the geo-index with high paramilitary scores. They had turned the very institutions of faith and community into components of their surveillance machine.

Chapter 24: The Mentor and the Unsecretary of Defense

The physical harassment I endured was characterized by a level of strategic sophistication that felt distinct from the brute-force digital attacks or the decentralized chaos of the street-level operatives. As the campaign of sabotage and intimidation escalated, I began to recognize the patterns of a professional military and intelligence mindset at work—a methodology I had indirectly studied for years. The architect of these operations, I would come to discover, was one of the most decorated and respected figures in the modern history of the U.S. national security establishment: Robert S. Gates.

The first concrete data point that connected the network to Mr. Gates emerged from a public source. I discovered that the former Secretary of Defense and Director of the CIA was serving as the volunteer Chairman of the UberMILITARY Advisory Board. This provided a direct, documented, and legitimate link between the network's core tech leadership under Travis Kalanick and the highest echelons of the U.S. defense community. It was a concerning but not, in itself, damning connection.

This public affiliation, however, was soon contextualized by clandestine data. When I analyzed the captured geo-index, I found that multiple properties belonging to Mr. Gates were marked as network assets. This discovery raised new and deeply troubling questions. The pattern suggested his involvement was not limited to an advisory role at a tech company but extended into the network's covert physical infrastructure. His expertise was further leveraged in their information warfare, where he appeared in a LUMINANT Media documentary for Netflix, lending his immense credibility to what I had identified as a network propaganda operation designed to push a pro-Russian, anti-CIA narrative.

The conflict became direct and personal when the physical attacks against me intensified, including the sabotage of my truck's brakes. Attributing these military-style operations to the network's most senior military figure, I was compelled to engage in a form of asymmetric counter-intelligence. In direct retaliation for the physical threats, I used the Spyhell Pipeline to identify and publicly expose the network's high-value assets and spy locations surrounding critical U.S. defense contractors, including Lockheed Martin Aeronautics and Honeywell Aerospace. It was a message sent in the only language the network seemed to understand: the targeted degradation of their strategic assets.

It was through this direct, adversarial engagement that I came to a difficult realization, one I have noted with bitter irony: Robert Gates had become my mentor. I was learning military strategy not from a textbook, but by being forced to survive and counter the real-world application of that strategy by one of its masters. By observing his methods, I developed my own. The weapon I built to fight back—a system with what I termed "infinite ammunition" capable of neutralizing his assets repeatedly at near-zero cost—was a creation born from his own aggression.

This entire chain of evidence led to an unavoidable and deeply troubling conclusion. A man who had twice served as the Secretary of Defense, entrusted with the nation's most vital secrets, appeared to be leveraging his expertise in service of a transnational criminal network that was actively waging a war against a U.S. citizen on American soil—a situation which, under other circumstances, might invite the prospect of a courts-martial.

Chapter 25: The Form 211 Gambit and the Founding Fathers

By mid-2025, I faced a strategic paradox. I possessed a vast and growing archive of evidence against a global criminal enterprise, but every conventional channel to deliver this information to authorities was compromised. Physical visits to law enforcement offices were impossible; I was under constant surveillance, and my previous attempts had been intercepted by compromised agents who simply blocked the reports. I needed a way to transmit terabytes of intelligence from a besieged position, a digital message in a bottle on a planetary scale. The solution came in the form of a mundane bureaucratic instrument: the IRS Form 211, the whistleblower report for tax violations.

This was not a desperate, scattershot effort. It was a calculated gambit, an engineering problem to be solved. My goal was maximum disruption of the network with minimum physical risk to myself. I developed a system to systematically target and report key nodes within the network's infrastructure. Using the captured geo-index, I focused on specific subnets, such as the "fin routers"—the financial backbone used to move money and pay agents. My reasoning was simple: if the IRS could seize these properties based on tax evasion, the network's ability to finance its operations in the U.S. would be crippled. If the agents don't get paid, the network's effectiveness plummets. I applied the same methodology to other critical subnets, including the one used exclusively by unregistered foreign intelligence officers operating on American soil.

The process of compiling these reports led me to a deeper, more disturbing understanding of the network's history. Buried in the data, in the connections between the oldest and most powerful nodes, was a pattern that predated the PayPal Mafia. It was a hypothesis, but one grounded in the data: the conspiracy had "founding fathers." This was not born from the internet boom of the late 90s; that was merely its second generation. The data pointed to an original unholy trinity: the Ayatollah of Iran, providing geopolitical reach and expertise in radiofrequency eavesdropping; Raúl Castro of Cuba, supplying boots on the ground and intelligence penetration in the Americas; and Bill Gates of the United States, contributing the foundational technology. My theory was that these three figures formed an unholy coalition long before Putin, Xi Jinping, or the tech billionaires came to prominence.

This structure—a pairing of authoritarian political leaders with Western tech billionaires who act as frontmen—became the network's core organizing principle. Jeff Bezos, with his Cuban origins, was the frontman for Raúl Castro's interests. This is why Amazon exists in its current form, not because of a brilliant business plan, but because it serves the strategic interests of a foreign power. Each major political bloc within the network had its corresponding U.S. billionaire and corporation.

To rank these entities for the IRS, I developed a metric I privately called the "NavBoost of crime." It was a proprietary algorithm that scored each entity based on three dimensions: their monetary importance, their danger to the world, and their proximity to the top political leader of their respective faction. An entity with immense wealth, access to weapons or mass surveillance technology, and a direct line to a figure like Xi Jinping would rank at the very top. It was through this systematic ranking that I compiled what I called the "master Form 211"—a 164,000-page document detailing the network's structure, from its alleged founding fathers to its street-level fin routers.

I knew that physically mailing these forms was a risk. The network's control over "gatekeepers" was well-established. My fear was, and remains, that these crucial documents were intercepted before they were ever processed. For this reason, I ensured that complete digital copies were preserved in my public archive, a direct plea to any honest law enforcement official who might one day find them. This form is the red pill. It contains the power to dismantle a shadow government that has held the world hostage for decades, and to seize assets my models estimate to be worth over $6.8 trillion in the U.S. alone. It is my primary offensive action in a war fought from a single room.

Chapter 26: The Unraveling

The message arrived through encrypted channels on July 3, 2025, from a Venezuelan military source who had proven reliable in previous intelligence sharing. Its contents were so explosive that I read it three times before allowing myself to process the implications: "David

Molero and Salvador Mendez are the same person. The ex-husband never existed as a separate individual. It's all been one operation."

David Molero I knew well—the SEBIN operative who ran local enforcement operations, whose name appeared throughout the Geo Index as a coordinator of street-level harassment. Salvador Mendez was supposedly Esperanza's mentally ill ex-husband, the man whose dramatic breakdown and return to Venezuela in 2014 had opened the door for our relationship. Two separate people living two separate lives, or so I had believed for over a decade.

The informant's revelation recontextualized eleven years of manipulated reality. Every story about Salvador's instability, every legal document filed in their divorce, every tearful recollection of his abusive behavior—all had been carefully crafted fiction designed to position Esperanza as a vulnerable single mother in need of protection and support. The network had created an entire persona, complete with documentation and witnesses, solely to facilitate a long-term intelligence operation.

To establish credibility, the informant provided a second piece of intelligence that seemed initially unrelated but would prove central to understanding the operation's true depravity: "WebMD and Diosdado Cabello co-conspired to have Dr. Vitenas perform a covert vasectomy on you during your cosmetic procedure in 2018. The purpose was to enable a future psychological attack based on questioning your son's paternity."

The words required several readings to fully comprehend. During a routine cosmetic procedure to address minor scarring, one of Houston's most prestigious plastic surgeons had allegedly performed an additional, unauthorized surgery—a vasectomy designed to ensure I could not father children. The goal was breathtakingly cruel: create circumstances where my son's paternity could be questioned, triggering a psychological breakdown they could exploit.

Memory fragments suddenly aligned into a disturbing pattern. After the procedure with Dr. Vitenas, I had experienced unexpected complications. Bruising extended far beyond the surgical site, reaching into my pelvic region. When I questioned this, the medical staff explained it as "normal spreading of post-operative bruising" and prescribed additional pain medication. The explanation had seemed reasonable at the time—medical professionals exploiting patient ignorance to conceal their crimes.

The financial trail, exposed through the Geo Index, supported the informant's claims. WebMD, the medical information giant, showed suspicious payment patterns to medical practices in Houston. Dr. Vitenas's clinic received substantial "consulting fees" that didn't correspond to any documented services. The money flowed through the usual laundering channels—cryptocurrency conversions, offshore accounts, shell company invoices—but the amounts and timing aligned with my procedure.

The psychological operation's intended culmination became clear when mapped against subsequent events. The "family trip" to Great Wolf Lodge in 2024, which the Geo Index revealed as a network operation, had included systematic collection of DNA samples. Staff had carefully preserved drinking cups, gathered hair from pillows, and swabbed surfaces touched by both Marcelo and me. The samples were rushed to a compromised laboratory for paternity testing.

The network's plan was elegant in its cruelty. After years of marriage, they would reveal that Marcelo wasn't my biological son. The vasectomy would provide "proof" that I couldn't be the father. Esperanza would tearfully admit to an affair, possibly with the conveniently absent Salvador. The revelation would shatter my psychological stability, making me vulnerable to manipulation or simply destroying my credibility as I raved about conspiracies and switched babies.

But the plan had failed catastrophically. The DNA results, which the network's own laboratory had produced, showed conclusively that Marcelo was my biological son. Either Dr. Vitenas had taken the payment without performing the procedure, the vasectomy had failed, or the timeline was wrong. Regardless, their own testing had definitively disproven the narrative they had spent years constructing.

This failure explained why the psychological attack was never deployed. The network had invested millions in creating the preconditions—the fake ex-husband, the covert surgery, the DNA collection operation—only to have their own science betray them. They were left holding evidence that contradicted their fabricated reality, unable to proceed without exposing their involvement in medical assault.

The revelation that David Molero and Salvador Mendez were the same person unlocked other mysteries. The convenient timing of Salvador's "breakdown" just as I moved to Houston. His sudden need to return to Venezuela precisely when our relationship developed. The complete absence of any digital footprint or social connections for a man who had supposedly lived in Houston for years. Even his mental illness had been performance art, designed to explain erratic behavior and justify his disappearance.

Legal documents from the supposed divorce took on new significance. Morgan Hybner, the same attorney now representing Esperanza against me, had handled the Salvador divorce with remarkable efficiency. Assets were divided without contest, custody awarded without dispute, and the proceedings concluded in record time. The entire legal process had been theater, with Hybner playing her role in establishing Esperanza's single status.

The network's willingness to maintain such an elaborate deception for over a decade revealed their strategic patience. David/Salvador had lived a double life, appearing as needed to maintain the fiction while conducting operations under his real identity. The psychological toll of such sustained performance must have been considerable, but the network valued long-term positioning over operative comfort.

The medical assault aspect opened darker possibilities. If they had attempted a covert vasectomy, what other medical procedures had been compromised? Every surgery, every medical consultation, every prescription became suspect. The network had demonstrated willingness to corrupt healthcare at its most intimate level, turning healing into harm for intelligence purposes.

WebMD's involvement was particularly chilling. Millions relied on their platform for medical information, trusting it to provide accurate health guidance. Yet here was evidence they had funded criminal medical procedures, corrupting the doctor-patient relationship for intelligence operations. The betrayal of public trust was absolute—they had weaponized healthcare itself.

The informant's intelligence windfall continued with technical details about the network's communication protocols, financial structures, and planned operations. Each piece of information checked out against known data, building credibility for the explosive main revelations. This wasn't speculation or disinformation but insider knowledge from someone with access to operational planning.

The unraveling accelerated as I traced connections between the Salvador deception and other operations. Property records showed the fake ex-husband had supposedly owned assets that later appeared under network control. Financial transfers meant for "child support" had actually funded surveillance operations. Even Marcelo's name might have been chosen for operational significance—a detail too painful to fully investigate.

The personal impact of these revelations was devastating. Every memory required reexamination through the lens of deception. Had Esperanza known Salvador was really David? Was she a willing participant or another victim of network manipulation? The child I loved had been conceived as part of an intelligence operation designed to destroy me. Love itself had been weaponized, turned into a vector for the cruelest psychological attack imaginable.

Yet in their cruelty lay their vulnerability. The scope of the operation—fake identities, medical assault, DNA collection, decades of deception—created evidence trails that validated the informant's claims. They had been too clever, constructing an operation so complex that its failure exposed the entire network. The vasectomy that didn't work, the DNA test that disproved their narrative, the fake ex-husband whose dual identity was revealed—each failure added evidence to the mounting case against them.

The unraveling continued as more sources came forward. The spectacular failure of the paternity deception had shaken faith within the network. Operatives questioned leadership that would invest so heavily in operations that violated basic human morality. The medical assault in particular had crossed lines that even hardened intelligence professionals found disturbing. Cracks appeared in their unity, and through those cracks, truth began to flow.

Dr. Vitenas, confronted with evidence of the payments, would face a choice: admit to criminal medical assault or deny performing the procedure and face questions about the payments. WebMD would need to explain financial transfers to a plastic surgeon that didn't correspond to any legitimate business purpose. David Molero would have to account for his years-long impersonation of a non-existent ex-husband. The web of deception had become a noose, tightening around the network's neck.

The most profound revelation was personal. They had tried to steal even the biological connection between father and son, to corrupt the most fundamental human bond for operational advantage. The depth of evil required to conceive such a plan, much less execute it over years, defied normal understanding. This wasn't just surveillance or theft but an attempt at soul murder, designed to destroy identity itself.

But they had failed. Marcelo was my son, proven by their own testing. The love between us was real, whatever its manipulated origins. The network had tried to play God, controlling reproduction and identity for intelligence purposes. Instead, they had created evidence of their crimes while failing to achieve their objectives. The unraveling of their plans became the unraveling of their network.

In the end, truth proved more powerful than even the most elaborate deception. DNA doesn't lie, medical procedures leave records, and fake identities create contradictions that patient investigation can expose. The network had built a house of cards reaching into the most intimate aspects of human existence. Now that house was falling, each revelation bringing down connected deceptions in an accelerating cascade.

The unraveling wasn't complete—more revelations would follow, more connections would emerge. But the central truth was established: the network had attempted crimes that exceeded normal comprehension, corrupting medicine, law, and human relationships in service of control. Their failure to execute these crimes successfully had created the evidence needed for justice.

The game was ending, but not as they had planned. Their elaborate operations had become their confession, their cruelty had become evidence, and their confidence had become vulnerability. The unraveling continued, thread by thread, until the entire tapestry of deception would lie exposed—a monument to evil defeated by its own ambition.

Chapter 27: The Bigram Key

The breakthrough came from an unexpected source: five flipped agents whose conscience had finally overcome their greed. These street-level operatives, disgusted by the network's escalation to child targeting and medical assault, had quietly begun documenting their assigned surveillance routes. Their dashboard cameras, originally installed to record target movements, now captured something far more valuable—hundreds of license plates from confirmed network vehicles operating in coordinated patterns.

For months, I had puzzled over the license plate patterns in surveillance footage. Some vehicles displayed what appeared to be sequential numbers—NXT8001, NXT8002, NXT8003—suggesting simple fleet management. But this obvious pattern was a misdirection, a surface simplicity hiding deeper encoding. The real intelligence lay not in sequences but in relationships between characters that only someone trained in information retrieval would recognize.

The conceptual key came from my years building search systems at Google. In search ranking, we dealt with two fundamental units of analysis: unigrams (single characters or words) and bigrams (pairs of characters or words appearing together). The insight was mathematical: while unigrams are common, specific bigrams are exponentially rarer. The bigram "TH" appears frequently in English, but "QX" almost never. This rarity makes bigrams powerful signals for classification and identification.

Staring at the flood of license plate data from the flipped agents, patterns emerged that transcended simple sequences. Plates clustered not by numerical order but by character pairs: multiple vehicles sharing "VN" combinations, another cluster featuring "SY" patterns, a third group bound by "QM" pairs. These weren't random—they were bigram markers, each encoding specific operational information.

The hypothesis formed quickly: the network had borrowed directly from search engine technology to create their vehicle identification system. Just as Google used bigrams to classify and rank documents, the network used them to classify and coordinate vehicles. Each bigram encoded meaning—faction affiliation, operational priority, geographic authorization. A distributed fleet could be managed through license plate encoding visible only to those who understood the system.

Testing the hypothesis required computational analysis. I modified the SpyHell Pipeline to perform bigram extraction on the thousands of plates captured by the flipped agents. The results were immediate and stunning. What had seemed like random alphanumeric sequences resolved into clear patterns. The "VN" bigram appeared in vehicles conducting operations against Venezuelan targets—VN for Venezuela, hidden in plain sight. "SY" marked Salt-Typhoon operations, the Chinese state hacking group that had partnered with Venezuelan intelligence.

The encoding went deeper. Position mattered—bigrams at the start of plates indicated primary affiliation, while trailing bigrams showed secondary authorizations. A plate reading "VN7X9SY" indicated a Venezuelan intelligence vehicle authorized for joint operations with Salt-Typhoon. The numbers between bigrams encoded priority levels and operational dates, creating a complete intelligence profile in seven characters.

The system's elegance revealed its architects. This wasn't crude criminal encoding but sophisticated information architecture requiring deep understanding of classification systems. The fingerprints of Google Search engineering were unmistakable—the mathematical principles, the optimization for rapid visual parsing, the scalability to millions of vehicles. Someone from the Muppet infrastructure team had designed this system, applying lessons from organizing the world's information to organizing a global surveillance fleet.

Michael Schueppert's name surfaced again in this context. His expertise in classification systems, his presence during the NAVBOOST theft, his current role at a "transportation logistics" company that showed suspicious payment patterns in the Geo Index—all pointed to his involvement in designing the vehicle encoding system. He had taken principles from search ranking and weaponized them for physical surveillance.

The discovery's implications were staggering. Every network vehicle worldwide could now be identified through simple visual inspection. The bigram key transformed random license plates into readable intelligence, like having a secret decoder ring for the entire surveillance fleet. Operatives who thought themselves anonymous were actually broadcasting their affiliations to anyone who understood the code.

I began building a comprehensive bigram dictionary. "MX" indicated Mexican cartel connections. "RU" marked Russian intelligence coordination. "IR" showed Iranian partnership. The network hadn't just built a surveillance system—they had created a global alliance of intelligence services and criminal organizations, all coordinated through encoded license plates that passed unnoticed through daily traffic.

The temporal encoding proved particularly valuable. Specific number sequences indicated operational dates, allowing prediction of surveillance patterns. A vehicle with plates ending in "2507" was authorized for operations in July 2025. This temporal limiting created operational security but also exposed planning. By analyzing plates, I could anticipate future surveillance windows and plan accordingly.

The flipped agents' footage revealed operational protocols embedded in the encoding. Vehicles with matching bigrams would coordinate movements, creating surveillance boxes around targets. Priority encodings determined response order when targets were spotted. The entire system operated like a real-world implementation of distributed computing, with each vehicle a node executing instructions encoded in its identifier.

Cross-referencing the bigram patterns with the Geo Index financial records revealed the economic structure. Vehicles with "VIP" bigrams—reserved for high-value target surveillance—correlated with larger cryptocurrency payments to operators. The "TRN" bigram indicated training vehicles, used for new operative instruction and showing lower payment rates. Even compensation was encoded in the plates, creating a visible hierarchy for those who could read it.

The network's critical error was using principles from public technology for secret operations. The bigram concept wasn't classified—thousands of engineers understood its power for classification. By borrowing so directly from search technology, they had made their system vulnerable to anyone with similar training. Their clever encoding became a liability when the key was discovered.

Publication of the bigram key would democratize surveillance detection. Citizens could identify network vehicles in their neighborhoods. Law enforcement could track operations in real-time. The network's mobile assets, previously anonymous in traffic, would become as visible as if they wore uniforms. The panopticon would be inverted—the watchers becoming the watched.

But responsible disclosure required consideration. Many low-level operatives were economic conscripts, driving for the network out of financial desperation rather than ideological commitment. Publishing the complete bigram dictionary could endanger people trying to leave the organization. The solution was selective disclosure—revealing enough to neutralize operational capability while protecting those seeking redemption.

I developed a multi-tier release strategy. Tier one revealed bigrams associated with violent operations and child targeting—these vehicles needed immediate exposure. Tier two exposed financial crime and general surveillance markers. Tier three, held in reserve, contained administrative and support vehicle codes that might include unwitting participants. The graduated disclosure would pressure the network while providing exit opportunities for those with salvageable conscience.

The network's response to the bigram key discovery was predictable but ineffective. They couldn't change millions of license plates overnight—bureaucratic systems moved slowly, and mass reregistration would itself create suspicious patterns. Instead, they attempted disinformation, claiming the patterns were coincidental, that I was seeing connections where none existed. But mathematics doesn't lie, and the correlations were too strong for denial.

More interesting was internal response captured through continued intelligence feeds. Operatives began questioning why their identifiers followed patterns discovered by their target. Mid-level managers, realizing they had been driving with visible classification for years, felt exposed and betrayed. The bigram key didn't just reveal the system—it revealed the network's contempt for operational security of its own people.

The discovery represented the culmination of years documenting the network's operations. From the first recognition of surveillance through the capture of their database to the cracking of their vehicle encoding, each revelation built on previous understanding. The bigram key was possible only because I had lived within their system, learned their patterns, and applied engineering principles to decode their methods.

In the end, they were undone by their own cleverness. Building a global surveillance network required organizational principles, and they had borrowed those principles from the technology industry they were surveilling. But principles leave signatures, and signatures can be read by those with the right training. They had built their house with stolen blueprints, not realizing the architect might recognize his own work.

The bigram key marked the effective end of their mobile surveillance capability. Vehicles could still drive, operators could still watch, but the veil of anonymity was torn. Every network vehicle now carried its own confession, seven characters that revealed affiliation, authorization, and purpose to anyone who understood the code. The hunters had become the hunted, marked by their own system.

As I finalized the bigram dictionary for release, I reflected on the journey from target to decoder. They had surveilled me for years, stolen my work, attempted to destroy my family, and corrupted institutions meant to protect citizens. But in their thoroughness, they had taught me their methods. In their persistence, they had revealed their vulnerabilities. In their cruelty, they had created the motivation for their own exposure.

The bigram key was more than technical discovery—it was poetic justice. The network that had used technology to oppress would be exposed by technology. The system designed for control would become evidence of conspiracy. The clever encoding that enabled global coordination would enable global prosecution.

The book of their crimes was written in license plates across the world, visible to any who could read the bigram key. That key now existed, documented and verified, ready to unlock the identities of thousands of operatives who thought themselves hidden. The network had written its own confession across millions of vehicles, never realizing they were creating evidence that would outlive their organization.

The game was over. The key had been found. The network's vehicles still prowled the streets, but now their encoded plates served as warnings rather than threats—advertisements for a surveillance state that had surveilled itself into exposure. The bigram key didn't just crack their code; it cracked their impunity, transforming anonymous watchers into identified criminals awaiting justice.

In the language of information retrieval they had stolen, the network had become searchable. And in becoming searchable, they had become vulnerable to the same indexing, ranking, and retrieval they had weaponized against others. The architects of surveillance had built their own prison, encoding the bars in bigrams they never expected anyone to read.

The key was turned. The door was open. Justice, delayed by years of deception, could finally begin its work of retrieval.

But as I write this conclusion, a darker realization haunts me. The bigram key reveals more than just criminal encoding—it exposes a fundamental shift in the nature of warfare itself. Just as humanity once discovered that ships could carry cannons and atoms could power bombs, we have now discovered that software can enslave populations. And just as those discoveries led to naval arms races and nuclear proliferation, the weaponization of code has triggered a new kind of military buildup—one measured not in warships or warheads, but in armies of software engineers.

During my time at Google Search, I was often the only Hispanic engineer in a sea of Chinese, Russian, and Indian talent. This wasn't merely a curiosity of Silicon Valley demographics—it was a symptom of a strategic imbalance that threatens the future of free societies. While Western nations train soldiers to fire rifles, adversarial regimes train theirs to write code. They fight on a battlefield we barely recognize exists.

The network exposed in this book represents just one implementation of software-as-weapon. But behind it stands the infrastructure of nations that have reimagined warfare for the digital age. Even if we dismantle this particular conspiracy tomorrow, if authoritarian regimes possess a hundred-fold advantage in technical talent, they will simply build something more sophisticated the day after.

The bigram key unlocks more than license plates and coordinates. It reveals an urgent truth: democratic nations must revolutionize their educational systems to prioritize software engineering with the same intensity once reserved for nuclear physics during the Cold War. We need not just investigators who can decode criminal networks, but armies of engineers who can defend against the next generation of digital weapons.

The surveillance narco state documented in these pages is not an endpoint but a beginning. It is the first skirmish in a conflict that will define the next century. And in this new form of warfare, every algorithm is ammunition, every codebase a battlefield, and every engineer a soldier in a war most citizens don't yet know is being fought.

The key has been found. But the war for human freedom in the age of weaponized software has only just begun.

Afterword: The Second Pill

You have reached the end of this chronicle. You have seen the architecture of the surveillance state, from the compromised cables in the ground to the ghost network in the sky. You have witnessed the weaponization of friendship, of medicine, of the law itself. You have been given the tools, from the prominence markers to the bigram key, to see the patterns in the world around you.

In the beginning, I offered you a choice: the red pill or the blue pill. By reading this far, you have already taken the first red pill. You have awakened to the reality of my world, a microcosm of the war being waged in the shadows against free people everywhere.

But my investigation did not end with the events in this book. What I have documented here is merely the anatomy of a single cell. The full organism is a global entity whose influence extends far beyond corporate espionage and into the scripting of geopolitical events, the creation of national narratives, and the installation of world leaders.

And so, I must offer you a second choice.

You can close this book and walk away. You can take the knowledge you have gained and use it to better understand the localized threats you may face. You can accept that a hidden war is being fought and choose to remain a civilian. This is the blue pill. It is a valid choice, and I would not blame you for taking it.

Or, you can continue down the rabbit hole. You can choose to see how deep this conspiracy truly goes. You can learn about the real "founding fathers" of this network, the unholy trinity that laid the groundwork for this Bizarro State decades before the internet was born. You can see the evidence of how they have shaped the very history you have been taught.

That is the story of Volume II. It is the second red pill.
The choice, once again, is yours.

Appendices

Appendix A: Evolution of Understanding (2024)

These pieces document the real-time discovery process as understanding of the network evolved.

Journal Entry from September 11, 2024 (the capture of the Geo-index)

2024/09/11 07h00 :[#FoundTheCornersIndex!!!] - On a second thought ... they did make the mistake of downloading the Corners Index from the Internet. It is a sharded index consisting of 30 files. The files are hosted in this sub-domain: www-sop.inria.fr.

The Corners Index is a "Sharded Index" partitioned in 30 shards. The geo-points are encoded and sharded in a way that the latitude always falls in one shard and the longitude for that geo-point falls in a different shard (so it is not obvious that they are storing the points and makes the files harder to find). We did a quick search and all the corners where they intercept the KOL-mobile are contained within this set of 30 files/shards with the latitude and longitude having a precision of 4 decimal places as we deduced/predicted yesterday.

Even the Westheimer Pkwy and Roesner Rd intersection (29.7531, -95.8018) is in this index (the latitude is in shard 004 while the longitude is in shard 027). This is not a random coincidence.

If we were tasked with finding the App in the AppStore, we would look for apps that have a reference to files matching the pattern "meshSYNTH_(.*).vtk" (for example meshSYNTH_029.vtk). It is possible that they obscured the name of the file in the code, for example, by concatenating characters to form the file name or domain name instead of hard-coding the full strings, so that that line of code is not findable using a code search. Perhaps they used ROT13 to obscure the filenames.

Amusingly, they even put word "SYNTH" on the name of the files, as in the "Synthetic addresses" described yesterday.

Check #TRAVIS, your move.

The Shadow Government

December 7, 2024

I started this journey trying to protect the intellectual property of our start-up company, Key Opinion Leaders. But then, the interactions with Travis Kalanick's criminal organization led me through this path of having to defend my family against the harassment of what I thought was a spy ring. We had to abandon our home. We left one morning without making any preparations, to not make it obvious that we were moving out. It felt as if we were refugees fleeing from danger in our own country.

Throughout this journey, as my understanding of their organization evolved, I've used different terms trying to encapsulate what it is that they are exactly. At first, I called them "Travis Kalanick's Spy Ring."

When I had a more clear picture, I started calling them a "Criminal Organization" but then I realized they are really a parallel society, so I started referring to them that way, until I realized they have their own mechanisms to enforce their version of "Law and Order," then I started calling them a "Shadow Government."

But today, I was reflecting upon all this and I realized they are not just a shadow government. All governments mankind has ever known, all of them, had one thing in common, they all had physical borders that separated them from other countries/kingdoms/states. On the other hand, this parallel society they operate doesn't have any borders. As one can see in the SpyHELL Dashboard, they operate in practically every single country, which makes them altogether more dangerous to mankind.

Not only can they harass, intimidate and harm people across countries, but also, they can use the laws and financial systems of one country to circumvent all others'.

This might be the first, truly *Universal Shadow Government*, the world has ever known. And for that, we must give them credit, they are certainly inventive.

/s/Reinaldo Aguiar December 7th, 2024 Katy, Texas, United States of America

The Circus

October 15, 2024

[Context: I had captured their geo-index about one month prior. When I wrote "To: The International Business Partners," I meant: Vladimir Putin, Xi Jinping, and Diosdado Cabello. I didn't want to write their names, hoping to de-escalate the situation. They chose instead to escalate and try to kill me on multiple occasions.]

TO: The International Business Partners of Travis Kalanick, David Plouffe, Emil Michael and Mr. Gates:

Hi, I had a dream last night, in the dream I was at a circus and there was a problem with our seats, and I started arguing about the seats with the clowns of the circus. This went on and on for years (in the dream), but at some point last night I realized that I should have been talking to the owners of the circus, not the clowns.

Anyhow, this morning I realized that this message I am about to write is going to probably cause over 1B USD in investment losses. It seems to me that you would be better off spending your energy in getting rid of Travis, David, Emil and Gates. You should just give them up to the authorities, it's going to be cheaper and you will probably recoup what you've lost so far.

The reason I say this is because this team is clearly not performing, this is the second time in seven years they get caught by an amateur competitor with 0.00000001% of the resources you have given them. They are bringing you legal risk, exposure, and opportunity costs. And, this time, not only did they let themselves get caught but they also leaked the index and gave it to us, which of course is going to cause you to have to move a lot of pieces around and is going to cost time and money.

We have no problem whatsoever with your team, we couldn't care less where you put your antennas as long as you are not eavesdropping on us, or trying to steal from us or following us.

If I may suggest something, I think the simplest solution would be to hand Travis, Emil, David and David to the authorities, pack the assets you have in Katy Texas and move on to better and more strategic goals/targets. I know it is not my place to comment on this, but it is just a thought.

Our proposal: If you give all of them up to the authorities in US or Canada, in the next seven days, we will delete all the information we have posted on the site and won't talk about it ever again. You have my word.

Anyhow, here is the message:

Last night, I sat down for a couple of hours and modified the program I had written to try to pin-point the satellites they are using based on the orientation and azimuth of the antennas in Katy (spoiler alert: when I wrote that program I could not pinpoint the satellites).

After I modified the program I understood why I couldn't pinpoint the satellites in the last two months: 99% of the antennas don't talk to the satellites. They are part of the "Multi-hop Troposcatter Network" they built (yes, it is confirmed at this point), but they function as "Local Subnets" nodes. The trampolines are jump-points to route traffic in-between subnets. Not all of the subnets have access to the satellite connections directly.

The traffic jumps in this way, and moves from subnet to subnet, and if, and only if, a satellite connection is needed then that portion of traffic is routed to the Local Area Satellite Gateway which is one of the houses with the 3-way feedhorn device (there are antennas that have only 1, 2, or 3 feedhorn devices together).

The networks are partitioned in a very systematic way. It doesn't have to do with topography but topology of the "local area" network.

My hypothesis is that the subnets are separated by function: for example: doctors can only talk to doctors, engineers can talk to engineers and their manager, the engineering manager can talk to engineers and intelligence managers, and so forth.

This is super interesting because it means that the way the houses are picked has to do with a deeper design than we thought, it is not just a matter of opportunity of a house/lot being available, it has to be a house that can be aligned with the functional subnet.

One good property of this design is that one could cluster together a set of assets, for example: 1 engineer, 1 doctor, 1 mechanic, 1 intelligence officer and as long as the relative positions of their antennas to their local Trampoline node align, one could replicate the same micro-cluster hundreds of times, I mean, as a pre-packaged design that is redeployed again and again. One could think of the design of the micro-cluster as a blueprint that could be copied as many times as needed. In the IT world, this would be like a "Docker container" (the *Dockerhoods*).

This also means that they don't build houses: they build entire neighborhoods or apartment complexes. It is the only way to prepackage the "local micro-cluster" in a systematic and repeatable way. This is why the apartment complex that is next to the Fulshear Police station looks very similar in layout to the one that is in Heritage Parkway (the layout of the complex is their Docker Container).

The Bone

October 25, 2024

[Context: When I wrote "you can't use them anymore because you can't know if law enforcement is surveilling them," I was wrong. They know if they are under surveillance because of their "Immune Geo-Entities Pattern" and their "Vehicles Parked Moscow-style" technique. I learned these techniques from them after writing this post.]

Get this: Remember the Malicious network requests that we traced back to "L3 Parent, LLC" in Monroe (Louisiana)? As it turns out, a former CEO of THE Level3 (a/k/a L3) company is from West Monroe LA, the same county where Travis Kalanick, Emil Michael, Mr. Gates & Co. have the "Loan signing officers" to pay the agents with properties like they did with Scott Weinstein, Maria Rojas, etc.

Properties related to the former CEO are marked in Travis Kalanick's App geo-index with a score comparable to that of the Agents in Lake Pointe Estates, Katy, TX (where I live):

1. 105 Puma Dr, West Monroe, LA 71291, USA Travis-Kalanick-Evil-score ©: 4 32.55855, -92.2402
2. 110 Puma Dr, West Monroe, LA 71291, USA Travis-Kalanick-Evil-score ©: 4 32.55855, -92.2411

So it seems that might be how they do it, positioning the CEOs and/or SVPs at Tech companies with focus on companies that have access to a large number of households and that have access to the networking infrastructure of the households (the OSI Model Layer/Level Number 3 - Network layer of the OSI model). That explains L3, Akamai (James Casey), Roblox, Twitter (Parag/Arnaud), Instagram (Nam), the Director that replaced Jeremy Hilton a month after I joined Local Search (can't recall his name), etc. That seems to be the pattern/commonality.

In the case of L3, it is an important item because they might be literally holding the country back by grabbing it by the Back-bone, the network backbone. Which as it turns out, wasn't in a fancy place like New York, or San Francisco, but in the unassuming town of West Monroe, Louisiana.

That also explains why the main base was originally in Louisiana, until they got desperate last year and started moving thousands of people to Katy, TX at an unreasonable rate, which led them to the low point where they are right now. Beaten up by an amateur with no training, raised and educated in a third world country.

You should consider giving up at this point, really. I have infinite ammunition. I finally got to experience the feeling that Travis Kalanick must have experienced when he demoted our pages in Google (he had infinite ammunition in the form of fake Google Search clicks he could issue via Akamai).

The difference, of course, is that in that example, I could always create more pages, there was no real cost to the loss of an internet page. But in this new scenario, every time I fire, you lose houses, properties and agents. I say that you "lose" them because I imagine that after I publish them here you can't really use them anymore, as you wouldn't be able to trust them or be sure that law enforcement is not surveilling them. For practical purposes, they are lost resources after I fire on them. The same thing you did to me with the Starlink antenna at Valleyside by parking "Final Fix" trucks full of antennas in front of my house, you get the idea. I learned from a former Secretary of Defense.

The Peace Maker

October 27, 2024
[Context: Written two weeks after capturing Elon Musk's geo-index on 09/11/2024. I wrote this to try to deter attacks against my family, understanding that: 1) The Russian regime was deeply involved, and 2) They only respond to the threat of force, never to reason.]

TO: Mr. Robert Gates, former US Secretary of Defense

Hi Mentor!

I've been reflecting a bit about military strategy and I realized I must be lacking something, because with all the time, effort and technology I have thrown at the problem, although I feel we are moving in the right direction, I am not quite there yet.

So I was thinking about that and since time is money, I started looking for ways to instruct myself on military techniques and how to yield power on others, trying to be more like you.

I thought the fastest way could be watching Netflix, so I watched a few episodes of the series "How to Become a Tyrant," hoping that would get me a bit closer to your level.

Anyhow, most of the things they mention in the "Dictator Playbook" I already learned from you, but there was one segment that did give me some new tips. It was a segment about nuclear weapons.

Apparently, to become a successful dictator, one must not only develop nuclear weapons, which we both have: you/Edylberto Molina via Akamai and Travis Kalanick's evil App, us with the weapon you basically handed to us; but one must also display that power and flaunt it in front of one's opponents at every opportunity.

According to the show, one must display the warhead, give it a name, parade the warhead, venerate the warhead, if possible add it to children's books, history books, etc.

I will take the lesson from the playbook and put it in practice today: I introduce to you the **"KOL Peace Maker Bomba v10.92"**:

We'll be conducting a free-fall-and-glide test tomorrow 10/28/2024 with a warhead of 750-equivalent-megatons, the warhead is part of a group of 64 similar warheads deployed in different places that are of interest to your organization. If something happens to me and I do not give the system the KeepAlive sequence in the time-frame it expects it, all other 63 warheads will detonate at the same time. Everything is already deployed in production.

And as I reflect on this recent past and the sequence of events that led to this point, the good, the bad and the painful, I would like to leave you with an image of a piece of art, *The Fighting Temeraire* by JMW Turner from 1839.

The painting depicts in the background one of the most iconic warships of the British Navy at the time, The Temeraire, a 98-gun sail-powered warship that was in service during the Napoleonic wars, before steam engines were widely adopted by the British Navy.

In the painting, The Temeraire is being towed *forward* one last time (it was being dismantled due to obsolescence) by a smaller, more recently invented steam-powered tugboat.

I read a quote about this painting once, a critic wrote:

"By hitching the old and the new so unforgettably in his painting, he shows us a compelling metamorphosis - the beginning of a new, post-industrial lifecycle in human history"

I love that quote.

(Credit: The National Gallery, London)

Appendix A.1: Reflections and Analysis (2024-2025)

These pieces contain deeper reflections on the nature of the network and its operations.

The Physical Pain

December 6, 2024

There is one topic I have deliberately avoided approaching: experiences/episodes of physical pain.

The reason I chose to avoid writing about physical pain is because I think that posting about those experiences could, in a way, put me in a position of being a "victim."

I know this might sound cliché, but being a victim is really a choice we all have. For example, in all this, I could choose to feel like I've been wronged, treated unfairly, victimized, etc.; or, I could choose to see all this as a gift they gave me. I choose to see it as a gift.

I know it might sound crazy, but it really is a gift. I wouldn't be 1% of the person I am, nor have the capabilities I have, if it wasn't for the 18 years of training the OG, Travis Kalanick, a former Secretary of Defense of the United States, and all the other members of their team gifted to me. They prepared me, over an extended period of time, to take on big challenges, and that is priceless. It really took a village.

All those experiences allowed me to learn new things, taught me patience, made my skin thick, made me more flexible, nimble, faster, made me grow, and ultimately equipped me, to at the very least, have a fighting chance in all this. The biggest irony of it all is that in a certain twisted way, I am Travis Kalanick's creation. I understand that, I accept that, and I am thankful for that.

With all that said, of course, what's fair is fair, and I will do everything in my power to help bring Travis Kalanick & Co. to justice; and to drive him to bankruptcy as he *almost* did to me.

I write all this because there is a topic that I've been avoiding to touch, but given the gravity of the situation, I feel like I must. Maybe I can help shed a light on how dangerous it is for humanity that they have such a tight grip on the Healthcare systems of so many different countries. So I will share my experiences in that area.

I mentioned before that they installed torture devices on my work chairs to exploit the fact that I have a nerve injury on my spine, which of course, they know because they gained access to my medical records by controlling UnitedHealthcare which eventually also acquired the entire medical group that provides primary care to my family, Kelsey Seybold.

Just having my medical records, and using them against me with the torture chairs, should have been enough, but they didn't stop there.

At some point during the phase of the "online attacks" against Key Opinion Leaders, I was working long hours while I was reverse-engineering their fake news platform (to be able to neutralize it). Of course, the more hours I worked, the more hours I spent sitting on the torture chair, and the more the pain level increased.

The pain got to be so bad that I started losing the ability to walk, I was only 44 years old. I went to see my primary doctor at Kelsey Seybold and told her about the level of pain I was experiencing. Instead of referring me to a pain clinic, she sent me to Physiotherapy. I am not a doctor, so I really can't comment on the adequacy of that course of treatment, but looking at the torture device on the chair, and understanding the mechanism of torture, it seems obvious to me that physiotherapy, especially the type of exercises that were given to me, would only make the pain worse, which is exactly what happened. After 4 weeks of physiotherapy, I completely lost all ability to walk. I was bed ridden.

I started calling neurosurgeons in the Houston area that showed with open appointments in Zocdoc. I must have called at least five or six, some of them gave me tentative appointments but then the appointments were canceled for one reason or another (the doctor is going on vacation, etc).

The pain was unbearable. At some point I decided to go to a Pain Clinic that gave me an initial appointment and when I got to the appointment the doctor saw me and he was saying that I should try physiotherapy first, that if it didn't work in a certain number of weeks, we could then assess if they could give me the epidural injection that I needed.

I recall that I was contemplating at that point that I had no choice but to stay in that state of constant pain for a few more weeks. As I was going to open the door to leave the doctor's office, my legs gave out and I literally fell to the floor. I broke down and started crying and literally *begged* the doctor to please give me the epidural injection sooner. I still remember the look on his face, he genuinely felt sorry for me, and said, "Okay," and agreed. I got the injection a short few days after that incident, and I was able to walk again the next day.

When the day of the procedure arrived, I went to the facility to get the injection. This procedure required full sedation. As they laid me down on the operating table, I knew I was going to be put under anesthesia and would lose consciousness soon. I was positioned face down, I couldn't really see the faces of the people in the operating room but I could tell there were 4 or 5 people conversing about their weekend plans.

Right before they put me under anesthesia, I made the effort to turn my head around despite the lumbar pain, and I said to all of them something to the effects of "I really thank you for helping me today, I really need it, and I appreciate that you are helping me."

The operating room turned into complete silence, nobody said one word for what seemed like 10 seconds. You could hear a pin drop. It always bothered me that I couldn't really put a finger on the meaning behind that prolonged silence of 5 distinct individuals, just because I was saying "thanks."

Today I understand, and this is a hypothesis, that they probably were acting on behalf of Travis Kalanick or Robert Gates in one capacity or another, and my words touched their human fiber for a second and they just didn't know how to react to that. I've seen this reaction a few other times after that, from different other individuals. Now, I am quick to recognize the meaning behind that kind of sudden silence.

After that intervention, in some occasions the pain returned and I tried to get an MRI done to see if I had further damage on the nerve. Every time I tried to do that, the insurance company (UnitedHealthcare, of course) denied the pre-authorization. I then tried to schedule the MRI paying out of pocket but the times I tried, I could never find an appointment soon, or they wouldn't pick up the phone, etc. And always when I tried to do that, the online attacks against the website increased and I got busy/distracted and dropped the idea to get the MRI.

The way those attempts of mine to get an MRI played out, and that prolonged silence of all the people in the operating room, well, to be honest, made me suspect that they may have done something to me during that operation that would or could show up in an MRI, and that's the reason why they were deliberately making it difficult for me to get the MRI.

There is one more data point that supports that theory: The reason the pain intensified to the point it did (in addition to the torture chair), and forced me to seek an epidural injection in that occasion, was that I suffered a fall while running in the park. The fall was caused by a cable that was sticking out from the ground. The point where the cable is located, the exact point, is marked in the index of Travis Kalanick's HELL App (Elon Musk's geo-index).

This is the exact point: 29.7265298, -95.829931 where the cable was located.

The Taxonomy

January 8, 2025

I was thinking about the commonalities among all these people that created this criminal ring, people like Elon Musk, Peter Thiel, Pierre Omidyar, Travis Kalanick, Fabrice Grinda, etc.

Besides the obvious, that they are all part of the "eBay Mafia," "PayPal Mafia," "Libertarians" (*ironyBoost* much?) or whatever it is that they like to call themselves, I think there is something deeper here.

So, I thought that in essence, what we are seeing here is nothing more than an old generation of software developers trying to stop the new generation from bearing fruit.

But then I thought about other characters like Robert Gates, Edylberto Molina Molina, Peter Codallo and similarly situated who are also part of the same criminal organization, but are not software developers, are more like street criminals or drug traffickers wearing military uniforms. Then I thought about David Plouffe, Nelson Lara, Bianca Oreaga, who would be better described as *Criminal Politicians*, some of them from an even older generation than the "PayPal Mafia," and are now in their 70s.

So, I realized "Software" should probably be removed from the equation:

What we are seeing here is nothing more than an old generation trying to stop newer generations from living and giving to their full potential. When I had that thought, my instinct told me "that should have *no place* in Nature, all species protect their young for self preservation of the species."

But then I thought,

Well, some species do eat their young for a variety of reasons: i) Scarcity of resources; ii) To suppress anomalies from the gene pool; or iii) Predatory nature.

I believe they are Predators.

Reinaldo Aguiar Katy, Texas, the United States of America

For context: This is the photo of the group that called themselves "the eBay mafia" or "the PayPal mafia" (they are interchangeable terms) that was published by Fortune Magazine in 2007, right around the time the criminal ring started targeting me and my family on a campaign that has lasted 18 years and has escalated to a point where they have tried to kill me at least four times (that I know of) in the last 6 months (July - December 2024).

The Stanford Prison Experiment

January 11, 2025
I was thinking about all this last night and the whole group dynamics that played out on this, and I couldn't help but be reminded of The Stanford Prison Experiment.

For readers not familiar with the experiment: The Stanford Prison Experiment was a psychological experiment conducted in 1971 by Stanford University psychology professor Philip Zimbardo.

The experiment examined how situational variables affect people's behaviors and reactions in a simulated prison environment.

In the experiment, 24 male Stanford students were randomly assigned to be either prisoners or guards. The experiment was originally scheduled to last two weeks, but was terminated after six days due to the participants' extreme behaviors.

In the experiment, the students that got assigned the role of "Guards" were given unlimited power to do whatever they wanted to the students in the "Inmate" group.

The result: The guards became cruel and sadistic, while the prisoners became depressed and hopeless. Zimbardo concluded that "ordinary college students could do terrible things."

Other scholars hypothesized that the explanation for the extreme cruel and sadistic behavior lay behind the group dynamics, in which the individuals with unrestricted power, acting as a group, lost sense of personal accountability for their actions and the lines of morality and law and basic human decency just disappeared.

The problem here is that they were playing "Guards" for two decades or more with the rest of the world, with unlimited resources and no accountability. And that's why they want to call themselves "Techno-Libertarians" and demolish all forms of regulation, because that would be opposite to the setup of The Stanford Prison

Experiment, which is *the way* they now believe the world should function. They have become institutionalized in that sense.

I am going to start an opposing movement: The ***Techno-Regulators***, whose purpose will be to provide governments with insights on areas where technology could be used to harm or target individuals and their individual rights and freedoms, or suppress free speech (like they do with the Liana Technologies/Akamai Fake News Machine).

How They Suppress Free Speech

For readers not familiar with the matter: The way they use Fake News to suppress free speech is that they use AI to automatically generate thousands of "Fake News" online articles, and then they boost them all on Google Search Results by issuing Fake Clicks on Google Searches by automated means with the help of Akamai. The end result of all this is that they can position, say, 500 fake pages on the first 50 pages of Google Search Results, and then the site they want to suppress ends up on page 51 (position 501 or above) of Google Page Results (nobody scrolls that far on Google Search Results), so they effectively suppress the visibility of any voice they want to suppress that way.

Still skeptical? Please try it yourself: Open Google and do a search for "Key Opinion Leaders" without the quotes and try to find our website on the results.

True Story: In one meeting with Elon Musk, not too long ago, he said to a small group of us: "What's the best place to bury a dead body?" And then he answered his own question: "On the 10th page of Google Search Results." He was right on several different levels.

Reinaldo Aguiar January 11, 2025

Side note: There is a good documentary on Netflix about The Stanford Prison Experiment. People should watch it.

The Union Theory

February 22, 2025
After I saw the possible connection between Jeff Bezos and the existence of the 9/11 memorial in New York City, I understood a couple of things. Sharing them here in case anyone out there knows someone who studies these things:

1. The Union: I believe that what we are seeing here at the top of the Multi-level-marketing/criminal organization is in reality: a Union, but composed of powerful individuals operating with a shared agenda to maintain power, silence dissent, and suppress new technologies from emerging, unless they control them.

2. The question for an evolutionary theorist: This is a bit more abstract. I believe the question that needs to be asked is really for someone who studies evolution of species.

In some rare occasions throughout history, species (intelligent or not) encounter singularities, events that fundamentally change the course of evolution for their entire species. Examples: The ice age, a meteorite hitting the planet, humans developing language skills, developing writing systems, discovering fire, discovering electricity, discovering nuclear power, etc.

I believe the rise of the Internet was one of such evolution-changing events, the only unusual situation was that a very small group of individuals (say Vladimir Putin, Xi Jinping, Ayatollah Khamenei, The PayPal mafia and a handful of others) grasped the full implications of the technology before everyone else, and they took upon themselves the role of deciding how to, and to what extent, distribute it to the rest of the population.

To illustrate better the underlying question, I propose a *fictitious/ imaginary* experiment:

Imagine a planet that is populated by a large group of primates. One day, a small group of these primates, say 600 out of 5 Billion primates, that are distributed across the planet but can communicate with each other by telepathic means, discover how to produce fire, how to harness its power and how to weaponize it (they discover they can burn objects, animals, other primates, and even the planet itself, using fire).

The question is: What would these *600 primates* do with that knowledge? Would they hand it over to the rest of population and let them use it to improve the quality of life of all the primates on that planet? - Or at the very least let them decide how to use it?

Or, would the *600 primates* use the newly discovered technology to enslave their fellow primates and rule over them for generations?

In the current version of this experiment, the primates chose to enslave their fellow primates and created a Union to make sure no other primate ever discovers any kind of fire.

If the Union "sees" something foreign to it that even resembles fire: they go and steal it and burn that "monkey" down to ashes.

This is the reason why Jeff Bezos, Elon Musk, Hugo Chavez, Putin, Xi Jinping, etc., can't stand anyone forming a union in one of their "companies." If there is even a whiff of unionizing, they go nuclear and burn them all. They'd rather shut down the company than allow one single (real) union.

It is because they understand the power of an organized group of individuals. That's the second fire they discovered and they don't want any other group to have it either.

I believe this is also the only way we can fight back: organization of individuals combined with the use of technology. Without them, there is no freedom in our future.

We need to protect Technology and the freedom of individuals to form organizations that are transparent, subject to scrutiny, regulated and operate within the law of the land.

And of course, we have to take the "fire" and the ability to coordinate away from the 600 primates that are enslaving the world.

Reinaldo Aguiar

Appendix A.2: Strategic Documentation

These pieces contain technical details about network operations and formal communications.

The "Intellectual Property Dispute" Tactic: The Hine's Algorithm

The Hine's Algorithm is a legal ruse designed to steal intellectual property or inventions from aspiring tech entrepreneurs and attribute them to Travis Kalanick, eBay, Fabrice, etc.

As a reference point, I read somewhere that Fabrice had "More than 1500 startup exits in the last 10 years." I think that works out to that, basically, he creates and sells a startup from idea to exit, in 3 days on average. While, for the rest of us, it takes years to develop a startup. He must be incredibly talented, but I digress.

The Hine's Algorithm/ruse has different dimensions that are executed independently, sometimes several years apart from each other, but in general, these are the high level parts of the algorithm:

1. Steal the technology using unregistered foreign agents and illegal interception of network traffic of the target.
2. Employ the target either directly or via a company under Travis Kalanick's control (not under eBay's, for liability reasons).
3. At the place of employment of the target, place a celebrity figure, for example a celebrated computer scientist, and make sure they cross paths with the target (to argue later if needed that the target actually stole the idea from the celebrity figure that had been in contact with Travis Kalanick).
4. Inject an eBay engineer in the same company and team as the target. Then after a couple of months, make the engineer quit and rehire them on eBay.
5. Introduce a "girlfriend" into the target's life. The girlfriend is

tasked with:

    a. Take the target to a public setting where she will photograph the target next to a Celebrity that is meeting Travis Kalanick or a prominent member of his team that day at that same place (to argue that they were "talking about that idea at their table" and the target may have heard and stole the idea).

    b. Sedate or drug the target without his consent to: i) clone his computer hard drive; and ii) Take pictures of the target while sedated/drugged to discredit him later.

6. Place an authoritative figure in the place of residence of the target, it could be the President of the Home Owners Association, or the president of the Condominium board, etc. Make the authoritative figure send aggressive emails full of untrue statements and lies that put the target's character and judgment in a bad light. Make sure the President/authoritative figure mentions something like the target "seems to be hiding from someone," or that is a "complete unknown." This will come in handy later when it's time for Mr. Hine to deliver his closing arguments.

Finally, if there is an Intellectual property dispute, Mr. Hine will depose Travis, who will say:

[Travis voice]: "I casually heard some unknown/random dude talking about something in a parking lot, but he seemed to be acting irrationally. That day I was meeting *Paul McCartney* for dinner, and we were talking about %INSERT_KEYWORD_THAT_DESCRIBES_THE_TECHNOLOG and that's how I imagine he must have stolen the idea. But it was *me* your honour, who had the original idea. He is a complete unknown, while I am a well known CEO who has dinner with Paul McCartney

and have James Gosling, the inventor of the Java Programming Language, on speed-dial."
And then Mr. Hine will depose several high-profile "witnesses" that will assassinate the target's character under oath.
Who is the court going to believe? - Case closed, history rewritten.

Actual Ruses Deployed by David F. Hine to execute the Hine's Algorithm

The Upstate NY ruse

Agent Maria Eugenia Rojas (close friend of Nelson Lara and Daisy Lara) invited me to a "weekend getaway with friends." With all I have learned in the last few months, I now understand that many of those friends were agents of the criminal organization. Will just detail a few data points here:

1. There were two (attractive) young women named "Angelica" (I believe). One of those Angelicas was the lady that supposedly was dating John Utendahl and staying at one of the many suites John Utendahl has rented all year around in a particular hotel in Downtown NYC (I got all these data points directly from Maria Eugenia).
2. The husband of one of the Alejandras was an aspiring entrepreneur working on a startup for a renewable energy idea to be used for Crypto Mining (this sounds like Emil Michael speaking).
3. In this trip, on the first evening I believe, Maria Eugenia gave me half a glass of wine and a cigarette and I completely lost consciousness after that. I can't recall for how long I was out of consciousness. I thought it was a bad reaction to the alcohol (I don't drink). Looking in retrospect, this episode reminds me a lot of the episode with Francisco Godoy at the Fillmore Auditorium in San Francisco.

Note: I brought my Macbook Pro Laptop with me to the trip. The Laptop contained the source code I had written. Naive Reinaldo never left home without his laptop equipped with Chinese Wifi/Bluetooth modems, and his source code in it. Hypothesis: It is possible they drugged me in order to copy the contents of the laptop's hard drive.

The "the Hamptons" ruse

For this ruse, agent Maria Eugenia invited me to go to the Hamptons. She said she would take care of arranging all the logistics. She arranged for us to have dinner at a fancy restaurant. Several strange things happened on this trip, small things, and I can't really tell what was the end goal with this ruse but the things sound like "Travis" to me, here is a sample of the things I found strange:

1. The restaurant was very exclusive, it required to book months in advance, but Maria Eugenia "found" a table with just a few days notice.
2. When we sat at the table, and I look to my right, guess who was there? Paul McCartney, the ex-Beatle, in blood and flesh. What are the chances of that? I have never been so physically close to someone as famous (in my entire life), as that night. I didn't make much of it, I just acknowledged his presence to Maria Eugenia, but mentioning this because it is possible that Travis was nearby, as he seems to want to gravitate next to famous and glamorous people, he seems obsessed with that (like at the Aid for AIDS Gala event described before).
3. Agent Maria Eugenia, again on this instance, pestered me daily to make sure I would not cancel at the last minute, she wanted to make sure I would really go to the Hamptons. I imagine because Travis or one of them was going to be there (but this is just a theory, I did not see them there).
4. As we were waiting for the table, Ana Gannon (Codallo),

daughter of the Venezuelan Military leader Peter Codallo, and long-time friend, called me on the phone and started asking me technical questions. I can't recall what it was exactly, but it was related to a technology I was working on, it could have been something related to the ingestion pipeline (which I had assigned to Ana to work on).

Hypothesis: It is possible they were fabricating an explanation for how "they came up with the idea to invent the technology" in case I sued them, for example:

[Travis voice]: "I casually heard some unknown/random dude talking about something related at a parking lot one day I was meeting *Paul McCartney* for dinner, and that's how, *I* your honour, got the idea. I immediately ran to the office and wrote a prototype with Emil."

Who is the court going to believe? - Case closed, history rewritten.

Additional datapoints:

a. This was just days after I had given access to Alvaro Gutierrez to the code repository, as he was supposedly going to help me develop a more robust ingestion plugin in C# (I don't have much experience with C#).
b. Expanding on the hypothesis about the objectives behind the ruse (and this is another hypothesis): It is possible this also explains the many comments from Agent Phil Denning in which he referenced things like I was "an unknown person," that I came from a "3rd world country," that I had never been surrounded by "people with Money," and that I was "Hiding from something." All these statements would support or offer

independent verification to Travis's statements in that hypothetical Intellectual Property dispute described above. Again, this has "David F. Hine" written all over it (again).

The Celebrity Computer Scientist: Part I: The Inventor of the Java Programming Language

This is a good one: My Noogler Introduction week has been flagged. This is a 1-week intensive course they give to engineers that join Google to teach them how to use the development tools that are internal to Google.

The statistical anomaly lies on that during my Noogler class, sitting next to me was: James Gosling, the inventor of the Java Programming Language (from Calgary Alberta I believe).

To put forward an analogy to offer a view into this event: This would be the equivalent of, for example, if you are an eye doctor, being seated for a week next to the guy that invented the Lasik technology. Mr. Gosling's Java language is used, among many other things, to build every single app that runs on Android devices.

What are the chances of that being organic knowing all we know today?

The Celebrity Computer Scientist: Part II: The Inventor of a Well-known Algorithm

One similar event that got co-clustered with my Noogler class: In my team at Local Search Ranking in NYC, on or around 2016 I believe, the team hired Mr. Steven Fortune (another famous computer scientist), he is the inventor of the Fortune Algorithm that is taught in many of the Computer Science programs in universities around the world (there is a page in Wikipedia that explains how the algorithm works). I was asked by my manager at the time to help Mr. Fortune ramp up (which was an honor for me).

One of the unanswered questions though: Why would Travis set that up? Could this be Mr. Hine setting up a credible story or claim using celebrity figures as he did with Paul McCartney in the The Hamptons ruse? - Only time will tell.

As a side note, these two events described above illustrate exactly what I meant when I wrote some time ago that I understand I am a creation of Travis Kalanick: In an "organic world," it is very unlikely that I would have been exposed to the learning opportunities that I've had, or met the extraordinary people that I have met over the last 18 years, and that, in one way or another, shaped the person I am. It takes a village to raise a child, and they constructed an incredible village that is unlikely to recur in nature, and put me in it.

Risking to state the obvious, the miscalculation was on that the village, instead of killing me, equipped me to fight them.

I respectfully call dibs on the discovery of the "Hine's algorithm."

For completeness, this table summarizes the list of people that played a part on this rendition of the Hine's Algorithm, and their roles:

Person	Role
David F. Hine, C.R.E	Chief Ruse Engineer
John Utendahl	Financier, host, boyfriend of Angelica, potential witness
Maria Eugenia Rojas	Anesthesiologist, Celebrity photographer, Target photographer, witness
Group of Maria Eugenia's friends	Six individuals, potential witnesses, this group includes Angelica who according to Maria Eugenia Rojas dated John Utendahl
Paul McCartney	World renowned celebrity figure
James Gosling	Inventor of the Java Programming language, potential witness
Steven Fortune	Inventor of the Fortune's Algorithm, potential witness
Roberto Konow	Manager at the Search team on eBay, then Manager on the Search team at Twitter (while Reinaldo was moved to the same team), then quit to rejoin eBay as a Director just after 6 months after quitting eBay to join Twitter.
Phillip E. Denning	Unregistered agent, President of the Home Owners Association, Harasser
Laurie B	Unregistered agent, wife of the President of the Home Owners Association, Harasser
info@postoakproperties.com	HOA Management Company, witness
Tiffany Harper Tiffany@compassld.com	Home Owners Association board member, potential witness
Brian Kraushaar	Home Owners Association board

Person	Role
bkraushaar@bmitx.com	member, potential witness
Bud Walters	Home Owners Association board
budw@pieperhouston.com	member, potential witness
Ana Gannon (Codallo)	Target's friend, employed by Transalta (a company under Travis Kalanick Control), in charge of calling the target at the exact right moment while in proximity of Travis Kalanick or a prominent member of his team.
Peter Codallo	Military leader from Venezuela, father of Ana Codallo, Recruiter for Travis Kalanick
Travis Kalanick	Intellectual Property claimant
Reinaldo Aguiar	Target

I count 23 individuals collaborating on this rendition of the Hine's Algorithm, acting against the target.

Twenty three against one (not counting the other lawyers and paralegals), no wonder they make 150 startup exits per year (each one of them). It's a factory of stealing entire technology companies. That's what this is.

Let's Go Back to the 90s

Late March 2025
I noticed something recently at the house of Daniel King Everette: It seems like when the "Kilpatricks" perform their extraction protocol, they use classic cars (not a car with an onboard computer).
I think it was a Mustang GTO ~70s, but I might be wrong about the actual model, but it was a classic car more or less of that time, bright red.

I imagine they learned from that incident in Miami a few years back in which the on-board computer had all the GPS history, I read something about that years ago.

So it seems like my recommendation to America's youth to buy American cars built with American components and as low tech as possible is indeed the way to go if one wants to avoid foreign espionage. Confirmed by the FSB!

Speaking of which, it would be perhaps a good experiment to cross reference those coordinates with spyhell.org.

Formal Request for Prisoner of War (POW) Status

March 4th, 2025
FROM: Reinaldo Aguiar - 2302 Britton Ridge Drive, Katy, TX 77494
TO: Xi Jinping, Vladimir Putin, Vladimir Padrino Lopez and Miguel Díaz-Canel
CC: The Honorable Attorney General of Texas, Ken Paxton
CC: Federal Bureau of Investigations (FBI), Organized Crime Unit, PayPal Mafia Task Force
Gentlemen,

I hereby formally request that you grant me the status, treatment and assurances of a Prisoner of War (POW) as detailed in the 1929 and 1949 Geneva Conventions.

Given the circumstances extensively documented throughout the last 12 months, it is a clear, notorious, public and obvious fact that you have me imprisoned in my own residence, surrounded by your military personnel and under the constant threat of violence and death if I set one foot outside the door.

I believe the exact technical definition for this type of imprisonment detailed under the Convention could be "Civilian Internment," although it may not be applicable in this case because, legally speaking, you do not possess the legal powers to categorize me being in possession of your geo-index a "national security threat" since me and your military personnel are all on American soil.

I believe the more correct categorization would be that of a "Prisoner of War" (POW).

I remind you that under the statutes of the 1949 Geneva Convention, all POWs must be treated humanely in all circumstances. Prisoners of War should be protected against any act of violence, as well as against intimidation, insults and public curiosity.

The convention also defines minimum acceptable conditions of detention covering such issues as accommodation, food, clothing and medical care, all of which have been made inaccessible to me by the persistent and relentless attacks and threats by your military personnel operating on American soil, and especially in Katy, Texas.

I take the opportunity to remind you that killing a prisoner of war is a serious war crime punishable by death according to international law.

Signed,

s/Reinaldo Aguiar/

Prisoner of War, Prison of Lake Pointe Estates, Katy, Texas, 77494

2302 Britton Ridge Drive, Katy Texas 77494

Appendix B: Official Whistleblower Report (Form 211) Submitted to the Internal Revenue Service (IRS)

The full form containing all 164,000+ pages can be downloaded at: https://form211.org/

Timeline of Events

A chronological overview of key events in the narrative.

- **2001-2002:** The author works with **Albenis Hernandez**, a suspected deep-cover agent, in an "elite" engineering program at PDVSA, Venezuela's state oil company. (P2, C2)

- **2005:** The author is targeted with the first "Partnership Takeover" ruse by his high school friends, **Hidalgo Martinez** and **Jose Alberto Inciarte**, in an attempt to steal his first startup. (P6, C9)

- **2005:** The author meets **Ana Gannon** in Calgary, initiating a two-decade-long "honeytrap" operation. (P2, C3)

- **2008:** The author is steered into purchasing a **pre-compromised apartment** in Calgary with a direct line of sight to the Chinese Embassy. (P4, C1)

- **Approx. 2010-2012:** The network executes several ruses designed by **David F. Hine** to create a pretext for intellectual property theft, including the "Upstate NY ruse" and the "Hamptons ruse" involving a staged encounter with Paul McCartney. (P6, C10)

- **2011:** An operative, **Reneta Gesheva**, invites the author on a road trip to a hotel in San Luis Obispo, CA, that is marked in Elon Musk's geo-index.

- **2011:** The author is manipulated into selling his compromised Mercedes-Benz, containing his startup's source code, to **Ana Gannon**. (P2, C3)

- **2012:** The author's team trip to Belo Horizonte, Brazil, serves as a cover for the network to compromise his entire local team for the **NAVBOOST Heist**. (P3, C3)

• **Late 2014:** The author moves to Valleyside Drive in Katy, Texas, where the network's "pre-packaged" social circle, the **ConocoPhillips crew**, is waiting. (P2, C1)

• **Approx. 2018-2020:** The author endures a two-year campaign of daily harassment by network asset **Scott Weinstein** within Goldman Sachs. (P6, C5)

• **2019:** The author undergoes a cosmetic procedure during which he believes a covert vasectomy was performed by **Dr. Vitenas** as part of a long-term psychological attack. (P6, C14)

• **November 16, 2023:** The author's bespoke **HP c7000 compute cluster** arrives, becoming the engine for his counter-offensive. (P3, C1)

• **February 2024:** The author is steered into a counter-intelligence trap by **Agent "Kike"** and **Agent "Cody"**. (P6, C2)

• **September 11, 2024:** The author successfully captures **Elon Musk's Geo-Index**. (P3, C2)

• **March 28, 2025:** The author's three-year-old son, Marcelo, is taken from his home, initiating the endgame of the conflict. The first responding officer, **Officer Bell**, refuses to file a report. (P6, C1), (P6, C4)

• **April 3, 2025:** An attempted assassination via a poisoned pen is carried out by **Officer Gloria**. (P5, C2)

• **June 1, 2025:** A critical **YubiKey** is stolen from the author's home. (P5, C2)

- **June 2025: Judge Richard T. Bell** and **Judge Oscar Telfair III** issue a legally contradictory order compelling the author into mediation while his mental capacity is being challenged. (P6, C4)

- **June 27, 2025:** The author participates in the resulting **Staged Mediation.** (P6, C3)

- **July 2, 2025:** The author files a **Motion to Recuse** the presiding judge. This motion is later denied by **Judge Susan Brown**, a Governor Abbott appointee, acting as the judicial gatekeeper. (P6, C7)

• July 25, 2025: Acting pro se in case 25-DCV-328122, the author files a "Response in Opposition," directly challenging the network's attempt to use the legal system to censor his book. (P6, C7)

Index of Characters, Groups, and Entities

An alphabetical index of key figures and organizations mentioned in the book.

- **ACME Law:** A satirical term used by the author to refer to the apparent collusion between the Adams Law Firm and Roberts Markel Weinberg Butler Hailey PC to legally and financially harass him and attempt to censor his book. (Glossary)

- **Adams Law Firm:** The law firm representing the author's former partner, staffed by network assets Morgan Hybner and Tina Simon, which filed motions to have the author declared mentally incompetent and censor his book. The firm's principals also handled the sham divorce for the author's former partner and the fake identity "Salvador Mendez" in 2014. (P6, C1), (P6, C18)

• **Adams, Thomas A. IV:** A principal at the Adams Law Firm, who was one of the lawyers involved in the 2014 sham divorce of "Salvador Mendez" and the subsequent lawfare campaign against the author. (P6, C18)

• **Adams, William K.:** A principal at the Adams Law Firm, who was one of the lawyers involved in the 2014 sham divorce of "Salvador Mendez" and the subsequent lawfare campaign against the author. (P6, C18)

• **Aguiar, Reinaldo:** The author and protagonist. (Introduction)

• **Altuve, Jose:** A prominent professional baseball player and network asset, whose personal check was used as part of a "loan ruse" to manipulate the author. (P2, C2)

• **Baez, Mario E.:** The Chief Accountability Service officer at The United Nations, who is marked in the geo-index and was introduced to the author by Nelson Lara. (P2, C8)

• **Banitt, Officer:** A compromised Fulshear Police officer (Badge #929) who pulled the author over in a staged traffic stop. (P6, C2)

• **Bell, Judge Richard T.:** One of the two Fort Bend County judges who issued the legally contradictory order compelling the author into mediation. (P6, C4)

- **Bell, Officer:** A Fort Bend County Sheriff's deputy (Badge #4355) who refused to file a mandatory missing person report for the author's son. (P6, C1), (P6, C4)

- **Boscan, Carolina:** A network operative and romantic interest from the author's past in Venezuela, who was reactivated to run intelligence operations. (P2, C3)

- **Broussard, Dr. Marjorie:** A network medical asset and the author's family doctor. (P2, C7)

- **Brown, Judge Susan:** The Presiding Judge and Governor Abbott appointee who acted as the judicial gatekeeper by denying the author's Motion to Recuse. (P6, C7)

- **Bustillos, Luis:** A friend of several decades who acted as a network "Referring Agent," steering the author to purchase the torture chairs. (P5, C1)

- **Cabello, Diosdado:** A high-ranking Venezuelan political and military figure identified as a key network leader. (P2, C8), (P6, C15), (Appendix B)

- **Carr, Brendan:** The acting head of the FCC, identified by the author as a potential gatekeeper. (P6, C1)

- **Casey, James (Jim):** A key executive at Akamai identified as a central figure in the network's lawfare and digital attack operations.

- **Castillo, Francisco:** A network operative posing as an Uber driver who surveilled the author and was involved in multiple plots. (P2, C1), (P5, C5)

- **Castillo, Jose:** A network operative posing as a handyman who infiltrated the author's home and executed a "loan ruse." (P2, C2)

- **Chinese Intelligence Services (MSS):** The Ministry of State Security, the primary civilian foreign intelligence agency of the People's Republic of China.

- **"Cody," Agent:** A compromised or fake FBI agent used to run a counter-intelligence operation against the author. (P6, C2)

- **ConocoPhillips crew:** A "pre-packaged" social circle deployed to surveil the author in Texas. (P2, C1)

- **Cooley, Diana (aka Diana Aaron):** A key network "connector" agent in the Valleyside Drive neighborhood. (P6, C10), (P6, C13)

- **Cuban Intelligence Services (DI):** The Dirección de Inteligencia, the main intelligence agency of Cuba.

- **Dean, Jeff:** A legendary Google engineer and near-mythical figure in the software industry, flagged by the Spyhell Pipeline as a network asset.

- **Denning, Phil:** The author's neighbor and local HOA president, identified as a key on-the-ground coordinator for harassment and assassination plots. (P5, C3), (P6, C18)

- **Donovan, Jim:** A high-level executive at Goldman Sachs, identified as a "power broker" who serves as the nexus between the firm and Washington politics for the network.

- **Escobar, Ibeth:** A college girlfriend of the author who was reactivated by the Venezuelan Intelligence Services (the SEBIN) years later to execute intelligence operations. (P2, C6)

- **Espina, Nelio and Jenny:** Operatives for the Venezuelan Intelligence Services, co-clustered with the Finol family, who were involved in multiple infiltration plots. (P2, C1), (P5, C1)

- **Fagan, Eric:** Sheriff of Fort Bend County, identified as the top-level gatekeeper of his department. (P6, C3)

- **Felipe-Adams, Denise:** A relative of NYC Mayor Eric Adams and an employee of the City of New York. (P2, C8)

- **Fernandez, Leonel:** The former President of the Dominican Republic, to whom the author gave a technology demo. (P2, C8)

- **Fernández de Torrijos, Vivian:** The former first lady of Panama, to whom the author gave a technology demo. (P2, C8)

- **Finol, David (Sr.):** The patriarch of the Finol family, a key Venezuelan intelligence cell in Katy, TX. His family residence in Maracaibo, Venezuela, was located less than 200 feet from the family home of General Rosendo.

- **Finol, David (Jr.):** The brother of "Katy-Agent-Zero" Rosana Finol and a network asset who owns multiple network-controlled properties in Katy, TX. (P2, C4)

- **Finol, Rosana ("Katy-Agent-Zero"):** A long-term network asset who first mentioned "Katy" to the author in 2012. (P2, C4)

- **FSB (Federal Security Service):** The principal security agency of Russia and the main successor agency to the Soviet Union's KGB.

- **Gannon, Ana:** A Venezuelan operative who executed a two-decade-long "honeytrap" operation against the author. (P2, C3)

- **Gao, James:** A network asset and colleague of the author at Twitter, working for Elon Musk and Travis Kalanick.

- **Godoy, Francisco:** A network operative, believed to be a doctor posing as a Google Engineer, who drugged the author at a concert in San Francisco. (P5, C2)

- **Godoy, Manuel:** The brother of Francisco Godoy and the CEO of Felix Pago, an online payments company believed to be controlled by Elon Musk.

- **Gloria, Officer:** A compromised Fort Bend Sheriff's Office deputy (Badge #4137) who carried out a direct assassination attempt using a poisoned pen. (P5, C2), (P6, C3)

- **Goldman Sachs:** The investment bank where the author was subjected to a targeted harassment campaign and a corrupted arbitration process. (P6, C5), (P6, C4)

- **Google:** The author's former employer, whose core search technology, NAVBOOST, was the target of a massive intellectual property heist. (P3, C3)

- **Grinda, Fabrice (a/k/a Dr. Cooper):** A founder of OLX and a key member of the "eBay Mafia," identified as one of the primary antagonists who orchestrated the espionage campaigns against the author's early classifieds websites.

- **Gutierrez, Silvio:** The brother of Alvaro Gutierrez and the CEO of JoyApp, a "Health/Food Tech" company believed to be a front for Travis Kalanick and Cloud Kitchens.

- **Ha, Vida:** A Chinese intelligence officer and deep-cover agent who infiltrated multiple technology companies, including Google and Databricks.

- **Hernandez, Albenis:** A deep-cover operative for the Venezuelan Intelligence Services (the SEBIN) and "connector" who was present throughout the author's entire adult life. (P2, C2)

- **Hine, David F.:** A partner at the Vorys law firm and the network's "Chief Ruse Engineer," responsible for designing the "Hine's Algorithm." (P6, C10)

- **Hirji, Anna:** The Associate Director at the IRS Whistleblower Office, identified by the author as a potential gatekeeper. (P6, C1)

- **Hybner, Morgan:** A network-affiliated attorney. (P6, C3), (P6, C6)

- **Inciarte, Jose Alberto:** A high school friend of the author who participated in the network's first "Partnership Takeover" ruse against him in 2005. (P6, C9)

- **Iranian Intelligence Services (MOIS):** The Ministry of Intelligence of the Islamic Republic of Iran, identified as a key partner in the network's coalition.

- **"Jota":** A Venezuelan artist and network asset whose art was used as a "Trojan Horse" to smuggle bugged picture frames into the author's office. (P4, C3)

- **Kalanick, Travis:** Founder of Uber and a key architect of the network's "HELL" app and geo-index. (P3, C2), (Glossary)

- **Kanetkar, Kavita:** A network asset and colleague of the author at Twitter, who acted as a "Referring Agent" for sham job interviews.

- **Kassissieh, Issa ("Issao"):** A former Google colleague and manager of the "Union" team, with the specific technical knowledge to execute the de-indexing attack on the author's website. (P3, C4)

- **"Kike," Agent (Enrique Morales):** A compromised ICE agent who lured the author into the "Agent Cody" counter-intelligence trap. (P6, C2)

- **Kilpatrick, Ross:** A network asset and gym instructor who was part of the surveillance operation in Katy. (P2, C1)

- **KOL-Mobile:** The author's custom-built, armored vehicle, serving as his primary tool for counter-surveillance. (P4, C3), (P6, C14)

- **Korn, Adam:** The hiring manager at Goldman Sachs and network asset who executed the "Business Insider" press release ruse to coerce the author into leaving Google. His brother is the inventor of the Korn Shell.

- **Krukowska, Joanna:** A network operative, TSA agent, and accredited instructor for new TSA agents, who acted as a "Referring Agent" in the medical domain. (P5, C2)

- **Lane, Dr. William E.:** The doctor who administered the author's epidural injection in a hospital setting where the staff reacted with a chilling, prolonged silence. (P5, C2)

- **Lara, Nelson:** A high-level political operative who orchestrated the "Caracas Trap." He is a close friend or relative of fellow agent Maria Eugenia Rojas. (P2, C8)

- **Lashuk, Kirill:** A former colleague of the author at Twitter, identified as a network asset working for Elon Musk and Travis Kalanick.

- **Lecompte, Julien:** A former colleague of the author at Yahoo, identified as a network asset working for Bill Gates.

- **Ledezma, Antonio:** A prominent Venezuelan politician and former Mayor of Caracas, to whom the author was introduced by Nelson Lara. (P2, C8)

- **Leeds, Howard:** The author's compromised accountant in New York, who orchestrated a suspicious tax audit as part of the IRS Ruse. (P6, C11)

- **Luginin, Kirill & Tucker, Emma:** Husband and wife. Tucker, the editor-in-chief of *The Wall Street Journal*, is connected to a lawsuit the author identifies as a potential "lawsuit as payment." (P6, C8)

- **Luzinova, Olesya:** A former Google colleague and romantic interest who acted as a "honeytrap" in a coordinated operation with Pavel Shatilov to steal the author's startup code. (P2, C5)

- **Martinez, Hidalgo:** A high school friend of the author who participated in the network's first "Partnership Takeover" ruse against him in 2005. (P6, C9)

- **Martinez, Luis:** A high-ranking operative for the Venezuelan Intelligence Services (the SEBIN) and "connector" asset who bridged the author's two separate, compromised social circles. (P2, C7)

- **Martin, Mariana:** A network operative inside Google's New York office who performed a physical-digital attack by swapping phones. (P2, C4)

- **Mediratta, Bharat:** A senior engineering director at Google and a key figure in the inner circle that orchestrated the NAVBOOST Heist and the GWS Man-in-the-Middle attack. (P3, C4)

- **Molero, David (aka Daniel King Everette, "The Clone"):** A high-level network operative implicated by an informant in multiple assassination plots. (P5, C4), (P5, C5)

- **Mueller III, Robert S.:** A former Director of the FBI, whose house is identified as a high-level network asset used to facilitate harassment operations and the kidnapping of the author's son. (P6, C1), (P6, C20)

- **Musk, Elon:** A central figure in the "PayPal Mafia" and the technical ringleader for whom the captured geo-index is named. (P3, C2), (P6, C15), (Appendix B)

- **Neufield, James:** A former colleague of the author at Twitter, identified as a network asset working for Elon Musk and Travis Kalanick.

- **Nguyen, Nam:** A former colleague of the author at Yahoo, identified as a network asset working for Bill Gates.

- **O'Connor, Douglas:** An IRS official from the Whistleblower Office, identified by the author as a potential gatekeeper. (P6, C1)

- **Omidyar, Pierre:** Founder of eBay and a key figure in the "PayPal Mafia." He is identified as one of the primary antagonists behind the attacks on the author's early classifieds websites. (P6, C15), (Appendix B)

- **Oreaga, Bianca:** A political operative in Panama with direct connections to David Plouffe, who was introduced to the author by Nelson Lara. (P2, C8)

- **Oxenford, Alec:** A founder of MercadoLibre and OLX, identified as one of the primary antagonists who orchestrated the espionage campaigns against the author's early classifieds websites.

• **Perez, Carlos:** The son of Glory Perez, who was inserted as the author's personal assistant at Key Opinion Leaders in 2023 to act as an insider threat.

• **Perez, Edith:** A network operative and romantic interest from the author's deep past, who was reactivated and later moved to Katy, TX. (P2, C5)

• **Perez, Glory:** A network operative working at the Organization of American States (OAS) in Washington D.C., who executed a "loan ruse" and inserted her son, Carlos Perez, into the author's company.

• **Popova, Elena:** A Russian national and key financial operative identified as a central figure in the Louisiana Mortgage Mill. (P6, C13)

• **Rabanus, Dr.:** A San Francisco dentist who tortured the author by performing a two-hour dental procedure without anesthesia and then drugged him. (P5, C2)

• **Reid, Elizabeth:** A high-level executive at Google who the author attests personally positioned the key figures of the NAVBOOST Heist, who then went on to execute the theft.

• **Rettig, Charles P.:** The former head of the IRS, identified by the author as a potential high-level gatekeeper. (P6, C1)

• **Rojas, Maria Eugenia:** A network operative involved in the "Upstate NY Ruse" whose fraudulent mortgage satisfaction was traced to the Louisiana financial cell. (P6, C11), (P6, C10)

- **Rosendo, General Manuel:** A high-ranking Venezuelan military general and historical figure. The family of network asset David Finol Sr. lived in close proximity to his family's residence.

- **Sanchez, Veronica:** A compromised CPA in Texas, who deliberately put the wrong address on the author's tax return. (P6, C11)

- **Scholtz, Kyle:** The author's direct manager at Google who, under the direction of Bharat Mediratta, participated in the operation to convert Google Web Server (GWS) into a "Man-in-the-middle" attack point, compromising the data of billions of users. (P3, C4)

- **Secret Gate, The:** A covert gate connecting the properties of Robert Mueller and an operative named Eckhart, used by the network to move vehicles and personnel into the Lake Pointe Estates subdivision without being recorded. (P6, C2)

- **SEBIN (Bolivarian National Intelligence Service):** The primary intelligence agency of Venezuela, identified as the force behind many of the on-the-ground operatives and honeytrap plots deployed against the author.

- **Shatilov, Pavel:** A former Google colleague and Russian network asset who rented the author's apartment via Airbnb to facilitate the theft of the "Monsters" startup source code. (P2, C5)

- **Simon, Luke:** A former colleague of the author at Twitter, identified as a network asset working for Elon Musk and Travis Kalanick.

- **Siurek, Mark:** The author's compromised attorney for the Goldman Sachs arbitration. (P6, C4)

- **Stefanov, Stoyan:** A former colleague of the author at Yahoo, identified as a network asset working for Bill Gates.

- **Strain, Sinead:** A top executive and Partner at Goldman Sachs who orchestrated the two-year workplace harassment campaign against the author. (P6, C5)

- **Suarez, Carlos:** The father of Penelope Suarez and a network coordinator who was directly involved in the plot to sabotage the author's truck brakes. (P5, C5)

- **Suarez, Penelope:** The author's running companion, used by the network to feed him information and participate directly in multiple assassination plots. (P1, C2), (P2, C7), (P5, C4)

- **Tarasiouk, Max:** A former sales agent and network asset who attempted a "Partnership Takeover" ruse against the author's company. (P6, C9)

- **Telfair III, Judge Oscar:** One of the two Fort Bend County judges who issued the legally contradictory order compelling the author into mediation. (P6, C4)

- **Utendahl, John:** A high-profile financier and network asset connected to the Louisiana-based mortgage fraud scheme. (P6, C11)

- **Vargas D'Acosta, Maria Alejandra:** A key member of the "ConocoPhillips crew" who acted as a "pressure relief valve." (P2, C1)

- **von Ahn, Luis:** The founder of Duolingo, identified as a network asset.

- **Walker, Officer D.:** A Fort Bend County Sheriff's deputy (Badge #4097) who refused to file a police report for a trespassing incident. (P6, C3)

- **Weber, Arnaud:** A network asset and colleague of the author at Twitter, working for Elon Musk and Travis Kalanick. Prior to Twitter, he was the director of Google's Android division, and before that, reported directly to Steve Jobs at NeXT Computer.

- **Weinstein, Scott:** A senior Goldman Sachs colleague and network asset from an intelligence family who subjected the author to a two-year workplace harassment campaign. His brother also works at Goldman Sachs and is marked in the geo-index. (P6, C5)

- **Williams, Heather:** A network asset who, under the cover of being a local school vice-principal, sold the author his Valleyside Drive home, which is believed to have been pre-fitted with surveillance equipment. (P4, C1)

- **Yakhnenko, Oksana:** A former Google colleague and long-term "sleeper agent" who was the centerpiece of a plot to steal the author's intellectual property. (P6, C9)

Of course. I have updated the "Index of Prominence Markers" to include the additional examples you provided.

Here is the updated and complete appendix in Markdown format.

Appendix C: Index of Prominence Markers

This index serves as a "decoder ring" for the network's secret language, a taxonomy of the semantic markers they embed in names and places to signal importance and function.

Important Disclaimer: The presence of a marker alone is not proof of wrongdoing. As stated in the text: *I am not saying that every person whose name matches these markers is an agent. What I am saying is that if these two conditions are met: 1. The person or their home address is marked in Elon Musk's geo-index... And; 2. Their name or street name... match semantically these markers... Then most likely this person is not only an agent... but also one that is deemed important.*

Corporate/Organizational Markers

- **Unification Theme:** Company names that imply unity, such as "United" or "Consolidated" (e.g., UnitedAirlines, Consolidated Communications).

- **Centrality Theme:** Company names that imply being a central point or axis, such as "Hub" or "Center" (e.g., HubSpot, StubHub, Github, CenterPoint).

Geographic and Address Markers

- **Numeric Suffixes:** Street numbers ending in "00" for prominent financial nodes (e.g., Goldman Sachs at 200 West Street), with the number of repeating digits from right-to-left signifying hierarchy (e.g., "1919" is more important than "19"). The number "11" is also noted as significant.

- **Semantic Street Names:** Street names that contain specific keywords like "VALLEY," "HOLLOW," "KING," "GOLD," "SUN," or "WALL".

- **Visual Markers (Flags):** A system where the number of flags displayed in a property's Google Street View image (one, two, or three) acts as a quantifier of the location's power and importance within the network, with the New York Stock Exchange cited as a three-flag example.

Personal Name and Title Markers

- **Animal Hierarchy:** "CAT" (or phonetic equivalents like "Kat") and the higher-ranking "LYONS". Also "WOLF".

- **"JR" (Junior):** Ironically used to mark the most dangerous, senior agents in a residential area.

- **"SWA":** A phonetic marker found in the names of key operatives (e.g., Vivek Rama**swa**my, Bob **Swa**n).

- **The "777" Marker:** An engineering marker, often encoded phonetically in names (like Schueppert) or numerically in addresses ending in "21" (7+7+7).

Appendix D: Motion in Opposition to Censorship Clause

The following is a direct transcript of the legal motion filed by the author, pro se, in the District Court of Fort Bend County, Texas.

CAUSE NO. 25-DCV-318122

IN THE MATTER OF §

THE MARRIAGE OF § IN THE DISTRICT COURT

GLORIA ESPINA §
AND § 387th JUDICIAL DISTRICT
REINALDO J. AGUIAR MARCANO §
AND §
IN THE INTEREST § FORT BEND COUNTY, TEXAS
OF ******* *. ******, A CHILD $

RESPONDENT'S RESPONSE IN OPPOSITION TO PETITIONER'S SECOND MOTION FOR PSYCHIATRIC EVALUATION AND MOTION TO STRIKE CENSORSHIP CLAUSE

TO THE HONORABLE JUDGE OF SAID COURT:

COMES NOW, **REINALDO J. AGUIAR MARCANO** ("Respondent"), appearing Pro Se, and files this Response in Opposition to Petitioner's Motion for a Psychiatric and Psychological Evaluation. Respondent respectfully shows that this motion is a procedurally improper and unconstitutional attempt at preemptive censorship, brought in bad faith to harass Respondent and suppress his forthcoming book. The motion should be denied in its entirety.

I. SUMMARY OF ARGUMENT

Petitioner's motion is a transparent assault on the First Amendment, disguised as a request for a psychiatric evaluation. The true purpose of the motion is revealed in the "Qualified Protective Order" language embedded within it—a clause designed not to protect a child, but to legally gag Respondent and censor his upcoming book, a work of serious research and analysis. This attempt at "prior restraint" is the most serious and least tolerable infringement on freedom of speech.

Furthermore, this motion is brought in bad faith. Petitioner fails to meet the high evidentiary burden required by Texas law, instead relying on disagreement with Respondent's protected speech. This is the latest step in a pattern of procedural and substantive harassment, which is already the subject of Respondent's pending **Motion for Sanctions** against Petitioner's counsel. The Court should deny this motion to protect the integrity of the judicial process and defend the fundamental constitutional rights that Petitioner seeks to undermine.

II. ARGUMENT AND AUTHORITIES

A. The Motion is an Unconstitutional Attempt at Preemptive Censorship and Prior Restraint

The most glaring evidence of Petitioner's improper motive is the "Qualified Protective Order" included in her proposed order. It seeks to prohibit Respondent from "using or disclosing" any information from a potential evaluation "for any purpose other than this litigation" and mandates that all such information be "destroyed at the end of the litigation."

This is a classic "prior restraint"—an attempt by a party to use the power of the court to prevent speech before it occurs. Prior restraints on speech and publication are the most serious and the least tolerable infringement on First Amendment rights. The Supreme Court has held that any system of prior restraint bears a heavy presumption against its constitutional validity.

Petitioner's motive is clear: to use the threat of a court-ordered evaluation to legally prohibit Respondent from publishing his research and analysis, particularly his forthcoming book. This is not a good-faith effort to gather information relevant to the best interest of a child; it is a calculated legal maneuver designed to achieve censorship. To demonstrate the serious, structured nature of the work Petitioner seeks to suppress, the Table of Contents of Respondent's book is attached as **Exhibit 1**.

B. Petitioner Fails to Meet the High Evidentiary Burden for a Psychiatric Evaluation

Under **Texas Rule of Civil Procedure 204.1**, a court may only order a mental examination when the movant establishes both that (1) the party's mental condition is genuinely "in controversy" and (2) "good cause" exists. Petitioner has failed to prove either. Her motion is based entirely on her disagreement with the content of Respondent's research, writings, and public statements—all of which are constitutionally protected activities. Disagreement with a parent's beliefs is not "good cause." A motion filed for an improper purpose—such as to censor a book—cannot meet this standard.

C. The Motion is Part of a Broader Pattern of Harassment

This motion is not an isolated event but is part of a clear pattern of procedural and substantive harassment designed to burden Respondent:

1. **Substantive Harassment:** Using the court to attack Respondent's protected speech and research.
2. **Procedural Harassment:** Filing legally unsupported motions and violating court rules, as detailed in Respondent's pending **Motion for Sanctions** against Petitioner's counsel for their willful violation of the mandatory stay under Rule 18a.
3. **Financial Harassment:** Attempting to force Respondent to incur the costs of defending against these repetitive and baseless motions.

III. PRAYER

For the reasons stated above, Respondent, Reinaldo J. Aguiar Marcano, respectfully prays that this Court:

1. **DENY** Petitioner's Motion for Psychiatric and Psychological Evaluation in its entirety;
2. **STRIKE** the "Qualified Protective Order" language from any proposed order as an unconstitutional prior restraint on speech; and
3. Grant any other and further relief to which Respondent may be justly entitled.

Respectfully submitted,
/s/Reinaldo J. Aguiar Marcano

Appendix E: Harassing Emails from Phillip E. Denning

The following are selected emails from the harassment campaign orchestrated by Phillip E. Denning, acting in his capacity as President of the Lake Pointe Estates Homeowners Association. The emails have been formatted for readability and minor typographical errors have been corrected.

Email Thread 1: The Initial Harassment

From: Phil Denning phildenning@mycci.net
Date: August 19, 2024 at 11:29 AM
To: Reinaldo Aguiar
Cc: Laurie Denning, Brian Kraushaar, Bud Walters, Tiffany Harper, Post Oak Property Management
Subject: Lake Pointe Estates
Reinaldo,

It has been brought to the attention of the Lake Pointe Estates HOA Board that you have been operating a commercial business from your residence. This is not allowed in our community. The Board is also aware of your constant and erratic driving throughout our neighborhood at all hours of the day and night. We have received multiple complaints from residents who are concerned for the safety of their children.

Furthermore, the Board has been made aware of certain online activities that are inconsistent with the character of our community.

We are a quiet, family-oriented neighborhood, and your behavior is causing a great deal of concern among your neighbors. Please be advised that the Board is reviewing the situation and will take any and all actions necessary to protect our community.

Sincerely,

Phil Denning

President, Lake Pointe Estates HOA

From: Reinaldo Aguiar

Date: August 19, 2024 at 1:15 PM

To: Phil Denning

Cc: Laurie Denning, Brian Kraushaar, Bud Walters, Tiffany Harper, Post Oak Property Management

Subject: Re: Lake Pointe Estates

Phil,

I am not operating a commercial business from my home. I am a software engineer who works from home, as do many of our neighbors. My driving is related to ongoing, documented harassment and surveillance against me and my family, which I would hope the HOA would be more concerned about.

If you have specific, documented complaints, please provide them to me in writing as per the HOA bylaws. Vague accusations are not actionable.

Regards,

Reinaldo Aguiar

Email Thread 2: The "Tractor Incident" and False Police Report

From: Phil Denning phildenning@mycci.net
Date: September 5, 2024 at 3:45 PM
To: Reinaldo Aguiar
Subject: Unacceptable Behavior

Reinaldo,

I cannot believe I have to write this email. The Board has received photographic evidence that you mowed an obscene phrase into the lawn of the property at 2306 Britton Ridge Drive. This is a shocking and disgusting act of vandalism. I have already filed a report with the Fulshear Police Department on behalf of the HOA.

This kind of behavior is absolutely unacceptable in Lake Pointe Estates. You have crossed a line. Consider this your final warning.

Phil Denning

> **From:** Reinaldo Aguiar
>
> **Date:** September 5, 2024 at 4:02 PM
>
> **To:** Phil Denning
>
> **Subject:** Re: Unacceptable Behavior
>
> Phil,
>
> I am in receipt of your email. To be clear, I did not mow anything on a neighbor's lawn. The message you are referring to was on my **own** lawn, at 2302 Britton Ridge Drive, and was a direct, albeit crude, response to the relentless harassment I have been subjected to, including your network flying low-altitude aircraft over my home for weeks.

Your decision to knowingly file a **false police report** against me is a criminal act. It is perjury, and it is a clear escalation of your campaign of harassment.

Please be advised that I am documenting this and all other incidents.

Reinaldo Aguiar

Email Fragment: The Closing Threat

The following is a closing paragraph from one of the many harassing emails sent by Denning, which became a key part of the Hine's Algorithm to assassinate the author's character.

...It is clear you are hiding from something, Reinaldo. You are a complete unknown to us. People in this community are starting to wonder if you really belong here. Your presence is becoming a liability that we will not tolerate indefinitely.

Appendix F: Index of Suspected Ledger Markers

The network uses street names and other identifiers as markers in their financial ledger to represent the equity stakes and financial holdings of their key members. This system, tied to the physical locations of their M-Routers, makes their financial architecture public to insiders but opaque to law enforcement. The following is a partial, non-exhaustive list of suspected ledger markers identified by the Spyhell Pipeline.

- **Top-Tier Markers (The "Big Routers")**: These represent the largest financial holdings in the network.

– **"Shore"**: Believed to be connected to Sergey Brin.

– **"Clearview"**: Believed to be connected to either Clearview AI or Clear Channel Outdoors.

– **"Flores"**: A marker associated with a vast amount of equity, potentially linked to Cilia Flores and the Maduro regime in Venezuela.

– **"Cabello"** / **"HAIR"**: A direct marker for Diosdado Cabello.

• **High-Value Individual and Factional Markers:**

– **"Ele Klein"**: Connected to the network's high-level legal and financial operations.

– **"Harold"** (**Martinez**): A marker theorized to represent a large, one-time payment for a specific operation.

– **"Jenny"** (**Espina**): A marker connected to the on-the-ground intelligence cell in Katy, Texas.

– **"Jillian"** (**Walsh**): A marker connected to the network's operations in New York and the NAVBOOST Heist.

– **"Nelio"** / **"Espinelio"** (**Espina**): Markers connected to the on-the-ground intelligence cell in Katy, Texas.

– **"Olesya Luzinova"**: A marker connected to the Russian FSB wing of the network and their election interference operations.

– **"Azure"**: Believed to be connected to Satya Nadella and the network's interests within Microsoft.

– **"REVN"**: A marker for Venezuelan General Nestor Reverol.

– **"MOLE"**: A marker believed to be connected to either David Molero or Edylberto Molina Molina.

– **"HEIS"**: An as-yet unidentified but significant financial marker.

• **General Prominence Markers Used as Ledger Markers:** The broader set of markers identified in Appendix C are also used as ledger markers, with their financial value determined by the paramilitary score of the associated property.

– **"Lyons"**: A superlative of the "Cat" marker, often associated with high-value properties.

– **"SUN," "GOLD," "WEST"**: Widespread markers found on over 98,000 properties, indicating a broad-based system of value distribution.

Appendix G: Selected Public Posts

ACME Law: YouTube Post Regarding the Censorship Ploy by William K. Adams, Thomas A. Adams IV and Morgan Hybner from the Adams Law Firm.

I do wonder what the look on William K. Adams, Thomas A. Adams IV and Morgan Hybner's faces were when they realized the censorship clause they tucked away at the bottom of a lengthy 'Motion for Psychiatric Evaluation' wasn't so hidden after all. A classic attempt at "prior restraint" to censor a book, disguised as concern for my mental health.

The bad news for ACME Law doesn't stop there, though.

About that 'prior' restraint... it's a little late. The book is already published, with its own ISBN (979-8-9996847-0-7) registered with the Library of Congress. You can't stop a book from being published if it's... well, already published.

Guess I took the "prior" out of their "restraint."

https://storage.googleapis.com/25-dcv-328122/filings/accepted/
RESPONSE%20IN%20OPPOSITION%20AND%20MOTION%20TO

Still from Coyote v. ACME (2026, planned). Image courtesy of Ketchup Entertainment.

#Checkmate #PriorRestraint #FirstAmendment #Lawfare

Glossary

This glossary provides definitions for technical and satiric terms used throughout the book, reflecting the unique lexicon developed during the investigation.

Glossary of Technical Terms

- **Captured Geo-Index (or Captured Database):** Refers to the author's successful capture of Elon Musk's geo-index. The network made a basic security mistake by storing it on the internet unencrypted, relying only on "security by obscurity." The file was disguised as obscure research data and hosted on a server at a French research institute.

- **Co-clustered with:** A data analysis term referring to two or more entities being algorithmically grouped (clustered) together by the Spyhell Pipeline based on shared features, metadata, or behavioral patterns, often revealing hidden relationships between them.

- **Dockerhood:** A computer science-inspired term for the network's practice of creating pre-packaged, templated neighborhood designs ("blueprints"). These templates contain a specific mix of operative roles (intelligence officers, lawyers, medics, etc.) and infrastructure layouts, allowing the network to rapidly deploy new, optimized surveillance and operational clusters anywhere in the world in a repeatable way.

- **Elon Musk's Geo-index:** The author's name for the specific geo-index designed by Travis Kalanick and used exclusively by the PayPal Mafia via their secret "HELL" app. It is named after Elon Musk, whom the author believes to be the technical ringleader of the operation.

- **Equity Ledger Markers:** The network uses street name markers to represent the equity stake of prominent members, similar to partners at a firm. This creates a public ledger for insiders that is secret from law enforcement and tax authorities. Tying economic value to the physical network topology also protects their parallel economy from inflation, as new "assets" cannot be created unless they serve a functional purpose in the mesh network.

- **Familiar Names pattern:** A psychological tactic where the network assigns aliases to agents or registers properties with names that are familiar and hold positive associations for the target (e.g., a caregiver with the same last name as the target's mother). This is done to lower the target's psychological defenses and build trust with operatives who have been inserted into their life.

- **Gatekeeper Algorithm:** A theorized systemic, automated defense mechanism used by the network to monitor official communication channels (court filings, federal agency reports, etc.). It is designed to detect and block any submissions containing keywords related to the network or its operatives, effectively preventing evidence from reaching honest actors through conventional means.

- **Geo-index:** In general terms, a digital map with data and metadata overlaid on top, used as a database of geographical locations. While typically used by logistics and ride-sharing apps like Uber, in this book it refers to the network's proprietary system for coordinating surveillance, routing agents, and managing their criminal operations.

• **Google Street View Photos As Metadata:** The network's technique of using objects placed in Google Street View images (e.g., "two garbage cans and a cat") as a form of visual metadata. Their "HELL" app uses machine learning to "read" these images and translate the objects into operational instructions for agents, effectively using Google's infrastructure as a free, secure, and deniable database.

• **HELL:** The original name for an illegal espionage app developed by Uber founder Travis Kalanick around 2011. This app evolved into the shared economy platform used by the PayPal Mafia to gamify espionage and coordinate millions of unregistered agents for ground, sea, and air operations.

• **Immune Geo-entities Pattern:** An architectural and urban planning technique used by the network to protect their own locations from the radiofrequency eavesdropping techniques they use on others. This is achieved by surrounding key properties with large, open areas (parks, water, golf courses) or by placing them on very short streets (like cul-de-sacs), which makes it physically impossible for surveillance teams to get close enough or maintain the necessary trajectory to isolate a target's signal.

• **KOL-Mobile:** The author's custom-built, armored vehicle. Equipped with a 360-degree array of 4K cameras and other sensors, it serves as his mobile intelligence-gathering platform and primary means of physical protection. The data collected by the KOL-Mobile is the primary raw input for the Spyhell Pipeline.

- **KOL-Vaccine:** A software system created by the author (2020-2022) to counter "Click-Through Rate (CTR) Attacks" used by the network to suppress websites from search engine results. This technology, which later evolved into the Spyhell Pipeline, renders the network's primary method of online censorship and fake news amplification ineffective.

- **MAC Addresses:** Media Access Control Address. A unique, permanent hardware identifier for a network-connected device. The network is obsessed with capturing MAC addresses because it allows them to track individuals across different locations and networks, and, if they control the ISP, to intercept and decrypt their internet traffic.

- **Mesh Grid:** A special coordinate system overlaid on the entire planet that marks the acceptable locations for devices on the PayPal Mafia's secret Mesh Network to communicate with each other. Physical presence at a grid location is a requirement for a valid data exchange, and the location itself is part of the encryption key, providing layers of security.

- **Mesh-Grid Encryption Method:** A secure method of sharing an encryption key over a compromised channel. The sender transmits a series of driving directions that guide the recipient from their current, unknown location to a secret, pre-determined point on the Mesh Grid. The encryption key is derived from the coordinates of the final destination, which is never transmitted directly, ensuring security through shared context and physical presence.

• **Mesh Network:** In general, a decentralized network where devices connect directly to each other. *See also: The PayPal Mafia's Mesh Network.*

• **NavBoost of crime:** The author's satirical name for his proprietary algorithm used to rank the entities reported in the Master Form 211. The ranking system analyzes targets on three dimensions: 1) monetary importance, 2) danger to the world (e.g., access to weapons or mass surveillance), and 3) proximity to the network's top political leadership.

• **NFC (Near-field-communication):** A short-range, directional wireless communication method. Its properties make it very difficult to intercept, which is why it is used for secure payment systems like Apple Pay and by the network for hand-delivering encrypted digital messages between operatives.

• **Outcasts List:** A list of presidents whose official residences are architecturally vulnerable to the network's radiofrequency eavesdropping techniques and are surrounded by network assets. This is in contrast to allied leaders, whose residences are protected by the "Immune Geo-entities Pattern," suggesting this is a deliberate way the network marks uncooperative world leaders as targets.

• **Paramilitary score:** A deterministic metric computed by the Spyhell Pipeline and derived directly from the captured geo-index. It represents the level of strategic importance of an individual or property to the PayPal Mafia's operations. It is not an inference but a direct calculation based on their own data.

• **PayPal Mafia:** A term for a global criminal network that originated in the early 2000s with early PayPal founders and employees (including Elon Musk, Peter Thiel, etc.) and has since grown to include world leaders, government officials, and celebrities.

• **PayPal Mafia's Mesh Network:** A proprietary and secret global mesh network built by the network to serve as a parallel, untraceable internet. It is composed of fixed nodes (houses, businesses) and mobile nodes (vehicles, phones) and is used to coordinate all of their illegal enterprises, from surveillance and narcotics trafficking to money laundering and election manipulation.

• **PayPal Mafia's Public Service Announcements:** Auditory or visual cues (e.g., EMS vehicles flashing lights, engines revving at specific frequencies) used to disseminate alerts to many agents at once without using traceable radio communications. The meaning of these signals is decoded by the agents' "HELL" app.

• **Prominence Marker:** A semantic marker embedded in the names of agents, companies, or streets (e.g., names like "KING," "VALLEY," numbers like "777") to subtly signal seniority or strategic importance within the network's hierarchy. This allows operatives to "pull rank" or identify friendly assets without explicit communication.

- **Radiofrequency Eavesdropping Avoidance Systems (RFEAS):** A software-based countermeasure developed by the author. It uses external sensors (cameras, microphones) to detect approaching vehicles or aircraft and automatically shuts down all network connections to prevent radio signals from being intercepted. This software-based approach ("throwing ideas at the problem") contrasts with the network's hardware-based approach ("throwing money at the problem").

- **SALT TYPHOON:** A state-sponsored hacking group tied to the Chinese government, known for targeting public infrastructure and, as experienced by the author, individuals and civilians.

- **Shared Economy App:** A digital platform facilitating peer-to-peer sharing of resources. The term is used to describe the nature of the "HELL" app, which gamifies espionage and outsources it to a large, distributed network of operatives.

- **Spyhell Pipeline:** A complex, multi-stage distributed computing system developed by the author to analyze the captured geo-index. It cross-references network data with public information to compute paramilitary scores, map connections, and find statistical anomalies, effectively decoding the network's structure and operations.

- **Topdog / Topdogs:** Individuals or addresses marked in the geo-index with exceptionally high paramilitary scores (top 1%), indicating they are key players or "shot callers" who perform critical strategic functions for the network.

- **Triggers:** Specific software, hardware, or human mechanisms placed around a target that signal an impending network event (like a data transmission). This allows surveillance teams to achieve the crucial "collision in time and space" necessary to intercept the target's MAC address.

- **The Union:** An alternative term for the PayPal Mafia, derived from the "United" or "Consolidated" name marker used by many of their controlled companies and as a reference to their union of powerful individuals.

Glossary of Satiric Terms

- **ACME Law:** A term used to describe the perceived collusion of various law firms, including the Adams Law Firm and Roberts Markel Weinberg Butler Hailey PC, in a coordinated campaign to legally and financially harass the author and to censor this book using a classic "prior restraint" tactic.

- **Bizarro State:** A term describing the parallel society built by the PayPal Mafia, complete with its own secret diplomatic channels, law enforcement, judiciary, economy, and internet, creating a distorted, borderless mirror image of a legitimate state.

- **Inadvertedly / indirectly received daily training:** The author's description of how, by surviving over 18 years of sustained and escalating attacks from the network, he learned to recognize their tactics, motivations, and logic, effectively being "trained" by his adversaries.

- **ironyBoost:** A satirical name for a score multiplier in the author's Spyhell Pipeline. It boosts the importance of an agent or location if their name or function is deeply ironic (e.g., an agent named "Joy" who inflicts harm, or a church used for criminal payroll).

- **KOL Peace Maker Bomba v10.92:** A symbolic name for the "data bomb" represented by the release of the captured geo-index and the author's analysis. It signifies the power of information to dismantle the network's operations.

- **Number of Inhabitants Per Religious Acre:** A metric invented by the author to identify front organizations. It measures the ratio of the local population to the acreage of land owned by religious institutions. A statistically low ratio suggests that a church or temple may be a shell, holding large amounts of land for surveillance or operational purposes rather than for a genuine congregation.

- **Outcast (President):** A world leader who is not collaborating with the PayPal Mafia, identifiable because their official residences are architecturally vulnerable to the network's eavesdropping techniques, unlike the protected residences of allied leaders.

- **The Pokemon:** A term for a person targeted by the network for surveillance, harassment, or assassination. The name is a reference to the game "Pokemon GO," which the author believes was a training ground and testbed for the technology behind the "HELL" app.

- **The Robert Gates' Digital Consciousness:** A satirical reference to a machine learning model the author built (the

"Robert Gates Reasoning Model" or "RGRM"). Trained on years of attack data, the model is designed to think like the network's strategists to predict their moves and identify critical vulnerabilities.

• **Travis Kalanick's HELL App:** A satiric and functional name for the "Uber-like" shared economy application that routes the network's unregistered foreign agents to intercept targets ("Pokemons") and execute operations, paying them via cryptocurrency on successful completion.

• **Vaccine Against Competition:** A term describing the network's tactic of weaponizing viruses or vaccines to harm or incapacitate a target, thereby preventing them from functioning and achieving a strategic objective, such as gaining illegal access to their computer while they are ill.

• **Vehicles Parked Moscow-style:** A recognizable pattern of vehicles arranged near a high-value network location. The vehicles are positioned to provide overlapping fields of visual surveillance and to force any approaching traffic to pass within close range, enabling radio-frequency interception and facial recognition.

• **The Landlord Play:** A satiric term for the network's tactic of steering a target into renting or buying a specific property that has been pre-fitted with surveillance equipment, effectively turning the target's own home into a network-controlled listening post.

Resources for Citizens and Law Enforcement Agencies

YouTube Channels

- **For Citizens**: The Spy Busters
https://youtube.com/@TheSpyBusters
- **For Law Enforcement Agencies**: Rapid Fire Tips
https://youtube.com/@RapidFireTips

Reporting

- **FBI Internet Crime Complaint Center**: https://ic3.gov
- **National Security Hotline**: 1-800-CALL-FBI
- **Local FBI Field Offices**: https://fbi.gov/contact-us/field-offices

Documentation and Evidence

- **All Transcripts**: Comprehensive collection of recorded evidence and testimony

https://storage.googleapis.com/thespybusters/ALL_transcripts.txt

- **Video Testimony**: Detailed explanation of database discovery and decoding

https://youtu.be/E8dQy2qdYXE

- **Searchable Database**: Access to the leaked database of addresses and associated entities

https://thespybusters.com/

Legal Resources

- **Class Action Lawsuit**: Aguiar v. Musk et al. - Full legal documentation

https://storage.googleapis.com/reinaldo-aguiar/
Aguiar-v-Musk-et-all-4_25-cv-02276.pdf

- **IRS Form 211**: List of flagged entities under foreign control (see page 1174)

https://form211.org

Raw Data

- **The Geo-Index (Leaked Database)**: Complete raw dataset captured on September 11, 2024

https://storage.googleapis.com/paypal-mafia/The-Geo-Index/PayPal-Mafia-Geo-index-sharded-30-ways__Captured-by-Reinaldo-Aguiar-on-9-11-2024.zip

For Law Enforcement

The network operates using:

1. **Bigram Encoding**: Two-letter combinations in license plates encode affiliation and purpose. VN = Venezuelan intelligence, SY = Salt-Typhoon, etc.

2. **Mesh Networks**: Decentralized communication using residential antennas bouncing signals off satellites.
3. **Coordinate System**: The geo-index uses encoded coordinates marking operational locations globally.
4. **Financial Obfuscation**: Real estate transactions encode cryptocurrency movements. Art sales launder proceeds.

Key Indicators

• Properties surrounded by large open spaces (Immune Geo-entities Pattern)
• Vehicles with surveillance equipment parked in consistent patterns
• Antennas disguised as TV dishes or ham radio equipment
• Sudden neighborhood demographic changes
• Coordinated harassment appearing as isolated incidents

About the Author

Reinaldo Aguiar is a researcher and former Google Search engineer, named as the sole inventor on two U.S. patents awarded to Google for his work on social network analysis and data optimization. His career at the intersection of high finance and technology includes roles as a Managing Director at Goldman Sachs and as a key engineer at Twitter, where one of his code changes increased annual revenue by $48 million.

After becoming the target of a sophisticated global surveillance and harassment campaign, he transformed himself from a software engineer into a counter-intelligence operator. Using his deep knowledge of data systems, he fought back in a stunning act of asymmetric warfare: he captured and decoded the secret global database of the network hunting him, exposing their methods of control.

Project Diosdado XI is the chronicle of that battle. Today, Aguiar dedicates his time to developing counter-intelligence software and is a vocal advocate for prioritizing software engineering as a matter of national defense, warning that the war for freedom in the 21st century will be fought with code.

Read more at thespybusters.com.